SCOTLAND'S CRAFTS

Edited by Louise Butler with photography by Shannon Tofts

SCOTLAND'S CRAFTS

Previous page
Bay at Luskentyre, Isle of Harris.

Published by
NMS Publishing Limited
National Museums of Scotland
Chambers Street
Edinburgh EH1 1JF

British Library Cataloguing in Publication Data
    A catalogue record of this book is available
    from the British Library

    ISBN 1 901663 42 6

THE SCOTTISH **ARTS** COUNCIL

Design by Mark Blackadder.

Printed and bound by Craft Print International Ltd, Singapore.

JEAN MUIR

Jean Muir was a founder member of the London Committee for The Museum of Scotland Campaign and her company, Jean Muir Limited, is a Founder of The Museum of Scotland. The Silver Treasury within the Museum is dedicated to her memory. This Gallery was funded by Jean Muir Limited together with The Goldsmiths' Company, The Incorporation of Goldsmiths of the City of Edinburgh, and Miss Muir's friends and colleagues worldwide.

Miss Muir was extremely proud of her Scottish heritage and her involvement with the National Museums of Scotland. As a prodigious patron, she actively encouraged and supported the diverse world of Scotland's indigenous crafts. Jean Muir Limited carries forward the traditions and standards of its founder. The company is pleased to assist with the publication of this most informative and fascinating book, and to see such wealth of creative excellence celebrated here today, as you will read in these pages.

Harry Leuckert
Chairman
Jean Muir Limited

CONTENTS

This book was originally conceived for an exhibition celebrating the traditional crafts of Scotland. What better time could there be than the start of a new millennium to take a fresh look at a part of Scottish culture which continues to enrich us, yet is often neglected in favour of more fashionable areas of the craft world.

This is not a nostalgic review, nor does it put forward a Utopian view of the traditional crafts. It looks at what kind of role these crafts play now and how they might survive into the future. It is also a record of particular crafts which are currently in the hands of a very small number of makers and which may, for social and economic reasons, disappear altogether. As in other areas of our cultural heritage, it is important that there should be both visual and written records for the future use of craftspeople.

These crafts have proved themselves stubborn survivors. Few are commercially viable today and rarely had access to state funding in periods when their 'amateur' associations and lack of the 'fine art' factor were seen as limitations. There are problems with obtaining the right kind of materials and tools in some cases and very limited opportunities to show work. However, in spite of such difficulties, the survival and, in some cases, revival of these crafts has been assured by the interest of a few committed individuals, by local groups and guilds, and organisations such as the Scottish Women's Rural Institute. For more than seventy years the Royal Highland and Agricultural Society of Scotland has been a loyal supporter of indigenous crafts through its Handcrafts Competition staged at the annual Royal Highland Show. The Competition has motivated gifted individuals to make and show heirloom items that may sometimes involve hundreds of hours of work. The production of, for example, a hand-spun fine lace Shetland Shawl is seen as a major challenge, or indeed as a lifetime's ambition. The very sociable nature of some of the traditional crafts has also greatly helped their survival and the past twenty years have seen an expansion in the numbers of single or multi-craft groups which offer not just friendship and support, but opportunities for personal development for many who have no art or design training. Latent creativity can emerge within the relaxed atmosphere of such groups.

Rosemary Wilkes

Previous page
Ring of Brodgar, Orkney.

This page
Westray, Orkney.

In the traditional crafts there is often complete harmony between the nature of the materials used, which may be local ones, and the finished article, and this is strongly attractive to makers who are concerned about environmental issues. No craft illustrates this better than basket-making and the revival of this craft has gone hand in hand with a widespread rise in environmental awareness. Considerable recycling goes on among traditional craft workers and there is a growing awareness of the toxicity problems of some materials used in the past, such as chemical mordants in natural dyeing.

I see both the exhibition and the publication of this book as very hopeful events since some of the crafts presented are now in a flourishing state with substantial numbers of people involved in them. Even the more obscure corners of the traditional craft world are periodically investigated by enthusiastic individuals drawn by the nature of a particular technique and who are not necessarily trying to make a living out of craft. The past is a resource that is constantly being mined for new inspiration and this initiative will, I believe, show that traditional crafts are very much a living part of Scotland's culture.

THE CONTEMPORARY ROLE

This collection of essays highlights a range of crafts distinctive to Scotland, examples of skills and goods that have their roots in Scotland's social, crofting and industrial past. These are the indigenous crafts, produced from a continuing tradition, using materials and handskills that have been passed on to or received from people across generations. Many of these crafts have a direct connection with working the land, fishing the sea, with community, subsistence, and a particular place, and usually they have a practical purpose. The crafts shown in this book bring to the fore only a small sample of the items that derive from this received heritage – part of a rich inventory which includes Harris Tweed, oat-straw kishies and Orkney Chairs, Ayrshire needlework, shinty sticks, kilts, fiddles, Fair Isle knitting and boats – all goods produced by intensive labour, made individually by hand or, in limited numbers, on small-scale machinery.

Contemporary traditional crafts are seldom presented in museums and galleries, save for examples from the past in social history collections, nor are they generally available to buy in high street shops. It is because this type of craft is so largely overlooked that it is important to bring it to wider attention before many of the intrinsic skills and patterns are lost. Some craft products are ordinary utilitarian objects – others, such as the quaich, are prized for special occasion or ceremonial use. This turned shallow drinking vessel with lug handles, originally made from bound staves of wood, is now more often crafted from silver, although a wooden version, the 'Bride's Cog', survives in Orkney.

Skills, materials and designs have not remained fixed in some bygone age – these essays cast light on aspects of current practice and developments in Scotland's crafts, posing questions about their continuation. Why bother teaching this to the next generation? What is the current value of this skill? What is its place, when associated occupations and grass-root industries have ceased or are in serious decline.

Many makers of traditional goods would not label themselves craftspeople; the articles they produce are merely part of their ordinary pattern of activity. The value they place

Louise Butler

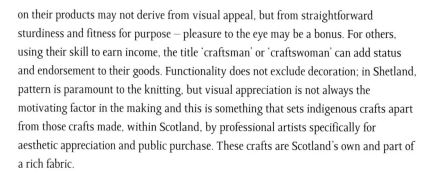

on their products may not derive from visual appeal, but from straightforward
sturdiness and fitness for purpose – pleasure to the eye may be a bonus. For others,
using their skill to earn income, the title 'craftsman' or 'craftswoman' can add status
and endorsement to their goods. Functionality does not exclude decoration; in Shetland,
pattern is paramount to the knitting, but visual appreciation is not always the
motivating factor in the making and this is something that sets indigenous crafts apart
from those crafts made, within Scotland, by professional artists specifically for
aesthetic appreciation and public purchase. These crafts are Scotland's own and part of
a rich fabric.

For some makers, the curiosity value of these individual crafts has presented new
opportunity, and recognition of commercial value has stepped up output, for example in
the Northern Isles, where Fair Isle knitting and model boats are sold as souvenirs and
gifts to cruise ship passengers and other tourists. Commerciality of crafts is still only
exploited to fulfil immediate needs and is just another facet of the increasing economic
importance that tourism plays as a means of earning a living in the remoter areas of
Scotland. No one is making a fortune from selling hand-produced crafts – but sales
contribute to the pattern of livelihood and income, often still pieced together as it
always has been in rural life.

In 1994 the Scottish Arts Council commissioned an independent nationwide report on
the indigenous crafts. This identified a range of traditional crafts skills still in practice,
showing which were thriving, although mainly as pastimes, and which still had a
commercial application. In contrast to mainstream contemporary crafts where many
makers are younger and possibly art-school trained professionals, more than fifty per
cent of traditional makers were found to be over forty years of age. Many had learned
their skill in childhood and had continued to exercise it throughout their lives – either
in a work or a crofting context – or had turned back to their craft as a means of
supplementing income in retirement, or after having opted out of an established career.
The option of a rural lifestyle, self-sufficiency and sustaining a craft is a greater

attraction to some than a guaranteed high income. Most would protest that their work is undervalued, but also realise that it is impossible to ask the true price for the investment of their time.

The textile crafts have largely thrived through wide membership of network organisations such as the Guild of Spinners, Dyers and Weavers, and rural groups. The incentives are the social gathering, the transference of information and patterns through published newsletters and the appeal of preparing special work for competition.

These skills are mostly practised as recreation; today there can be little commercial context for the amount of time spent, for example, in preparing a fleece, spinning and plying the wool, and gathering plants for natural dyeing, before knitting or weaving the finished garment or length of cloth. Even in Shetland and the Western Isles, where production of fine knitting and hand woven Harris Tweed are still living industries, yarn is chemically dyed, factory-bought, and cloth is sent away for finishing, even if it does come back to the croft for small-scale direct sale or to fulfil orders.

Where specific markets exist, a limited number of producers supply the need. Curling stones, golf clubs, camans (shinty sticks) are still hand-made — mainly for school, club and competition use. Musical instruments — fiddles, clarsachs and sets of pipes — are commissioned from individual makers by Scotland's traditional musicians — with a new generation of young musicians coming up through the Feisean movement of tuition-based festivals. Scotland's national dress, the kilt, is of unique significance and widely worn at ceilidhs and as wedding attire. Clients look to Highland dress outfitters, many of whom employ outworkers, or to individual master kiltmakers who hand-build their kilts — calculating pleats to the customer's height and girth and hand-stitching and finishing to precise measurements. Dress accessories, such as sporrans and sgian-dubhs, while often mass-produced, can still be ordered directly from a craftsman's workshop where pelts and leather will be selected by a discriminating eye, stitched and finished by hand, or metal tempered and finished to instrument precision.

Below
Lichen or 'crotal' was scraped from the rocks for use as a natural dyestuff.

Regional crafts are no longer exclusive to their original geographic locations; the media, special interest groups and involvement in national competitions have all played a part in promulgating Scotland's regional crafts. Several, however, remain localised in the hands of just a few practitioners – Eriskay fisher ganseys, at the southern tip of the Uists in the Western Isles, Sanquhar knitting in Dumfriesshire with its distinctive, graphic black and white geometric patterns, straw-back chairs in Orkney.

It is these localised crafts that are probably most at risk of floundering in the future. What is the incentive for those people, often elderly, holding rare skills in their hands, to pass on this knowledge, other than a very personal drive to do so? Fortunately there are individuals who have taken up this mission. On mainland Shetland, for instance, Lawrence Copland grows, crops and prepares black oats for straw, endeavouring to

provide enough material from his croft not only for his own requirements, but also to service the students at his seasonal kishie-making (straw basket) class. Near Kilmarnock, Agnes F Bryson holds occasional small classes to teach Ayrshire whitework – a delicate hand embroidery worked on fine cotton muslin, with decorative needlepoint lace filling stitches. From 1820-70 this type of embroidery provided a home industry for thousands of women in this area of Scotland, until its rapid demise with the advent of machine embroidery and the subsequent shift in fashion demand. It is quite telling that Mrs Bryson receives as much interest from embroiderers travelling from North America, Canada, Australia and New Zealand as from Scots.

In 1994 the Kilt Training School opened in Keith, Aberdeenshire. Set up in a refurbished textile mill in response to Highland dress distributors who were aware of the need to increase the number of trained kiltmakers to service the demand for traditional kilts, the Moray Council has been a major funding source for this venture, with substantial support from the European Social Fund. Course leader, Robert McBain, a master kiltmaker who perfected his craft as Regimental Kiltmaker to the Gordon Highlanders, annually leads around a dozen students through the twelve-month training, now validated by the Scottish Qualifications Authority.

In primary and secondary schools there is little evidence of Scottish traditional crafts on the timetable, save where a particular teacher chooses to include their personal interest within a general lesson. The Shetland Islands are an exception: Fair Isle patterned knitting is taught in all primary schools.

Area tourist boards and local enterprise companies have, in some regions, recognised the value of small home-craft industries to tourism initiatives and economic development. Makers are supported through inclusion in craft 'trails' which signpost a degree of extra business direct to the door, in many cases allowing visitors to make the connection between land, material, process and product. This encouragement and support has led several makers with unique products such as Orkney Chairs to realise a small export market, even advertising and selling through web-pages on the internet.

Advances in transmitting skills or raising awareness have occurred in regions where arts or craft development officers are employed, usually by the local authority, to work directly with the community and organise events and educational activities. The advocacy and communication role that these individuals play can be highly supportive. The growing membership of network groups, particularly in the areas of spinning, weaving and basket-making, and the active commitment of many makers may collectively help to give a brighter future to Scotland's own crafts.

From early times people in Scotland have used dyes to add colour to clothing and other textile articles. Historically, native plants have played a major role in dyeing, with traditional dyeing methods continuing to play a part until the present day.

Natural dyeing is a chemical process performed to fix colours from dyestuffs on to fabrics. 'Substantive' dyes bond naturally on to materials without additional treatment. Most dyes, however, are 'fugitive', requiring the addition of a fixative known as a mordant in the process. The dyeing process often also uses alterants that affect the final colour. Alterants are typically either alkali, for example washing soda, or acid, for example vinegar.

Dyeing using native plants can require significant volumes of materials, recipes often calling for an equal weight of fresh plant material to yarn. Many forms of yellow and green can be obtained from flowers, leaves and stems of plants, while browns can be obtained from the bark or roots of trees or shrubs. Fewer native species produce good reds or blues and there is a long history of importation of materials producing these colours.

Early on there was a divergence in dyeing practice as carried out by professional dyers in towns and by individuals who performed dyeing for their family and others in the locality. Town dyers, working with relatively large volumes of materials, more frequently used imported dyestuffs including madder (for reds) from early times.

The native flora would have been extensively used for dyeing home-woven plaid or kilts before the 1747 Prohibition of Highland Dress Act, introduced in the wake of the 1745 Jacobite Rising. Much knowledge of plant dyes was lost during the period of proscription, and after the Act was repealed in 1782 tartan manufacture became mechanised and employed imported dyes.

The manufacture of tweed, a material based on plaid, was already well established in the Borders by the 1830s, using imported dyestuffs in large-scale manufacturing

COLOURING
THE CLOTH

Doreen MacIntyre

processes. The development of the tweed industry in the Highlands and Islands started later. Introduced as a poor relief measure to Harris and Lewis in 1840, Harris Tweed manufacture continues to the present day. Until the introduction of chemical dyes to the Outer Hebrides in the late nineteenth century, the dyestuffs used were almost exclusively obtained from local plant sources. The species used included heather, flag iris, ragwort, and lichen (crotal). Imported indigo was used to provide blue. After the introduction of chemical dyes, the usage of plant dyes for Harris Tweed declined sharply, but a few weavers continued to dye in the tradition, a practice which has continued (although at an ever decreasing level) until present.

In general it appears that the users of plant materials were careful to ensure that the stocks of their dye sources were sustainably conserved, but there were some instances where over-extraction of plant material caused an adverse environmental impact. The picking of plants for their roots was forbidden by an Act of Parliament in 1695, a dictate that seems to have been ignored by those seeking ladies' bedstraw and tormentil for their dyeing and tanning qualities. Eighteenth-century records indicate the continuing removal of ladies' bedstraw from the machair (the flower rich sandy areas by the sea) in the Outer Isles, a factor that contributed to coastal erosion. The only well documented example of over-extraction of plant material for industrial purposes occurred as a result of collections carried out for a preparation of the red/purple orchil dye 'Cudbear' obtained from certain species of lichens. Established in Leith in 1758, the Cudbear manufacturing process had an annual requirement for around 250 tons of lichens. Initially the lichen stock was obtained from the Highlands and Islands, but the significant rate of extraction saw these stocks rapidly depleted. Subsequently lichens were imported from Scandinavia and other locations.

Several species of plants, along with other natural materials, were traditionally used in the production of mordants. Dock and sorrel were used to provide oxalic acid, bog iron was used for dark colours, and stale urine was used as a mordant and to soften the coarse woollen cloth.

Traditionally, the use of plant materials for dyeing was a secretive art. The knowledge of species, recipes and methods was handed down from mother to daughter, by example and involvement, not in the prescriptive way of industrial dyers. Some recipes were, however, written down and Fraser relates a case in the Western Isles where the recipes were kept in a locked chest, which was to be burned when the last owner had died without passing them on to the next generation. Dyeing in the traditional way was relatively common in some of the Outer Isles until fairly recent times. There are still a few older people in the islands whose dyeing methods are based on inherited knowledge, but the practice has all but died out, with possibly only one remaining practitioner still involved in Harris Tweed production using native plant dyes. The tradition was essentially a subsistence practice based on need and expediency, and once the islands became more economically buoyant there was a significant shift towards the less time-consuming and simpler methods provided by chemical dyes.

There was a resurgence of interest in natural dyeing during the 1970s and several present-day dyers became involved during this period. Today's dyers tend to be motivated by a personal interest in natural processes. Most people learn through reading books, attending workshops and networking with other dyers. They are mainly people who are keen to experiment and take the craft forward.

Many traditional species are used, especially those which are abundant (heather for instance) or considered weeds, such as docks, nettles and ragwort. Most dyers use chemical mordants, but in smaller proportions than previously. The rewards these dyers reap in their use of these materials include the pleasure of the natural process, the subtle blend of the colours obtained, and the sheer serendipity of the results.

During the 1990s there has been a growth of interest in dyeing using native fungi, from which a wide range of colours can be obtained. There are probably between 100 and 200 people actively involved with dyes from native flora and fungi at present. The dyers are involved in making a wide variety of articles – most with yarn and knitted items, but also with tapestries, weaving and rugs. Many pursue the interest at a hobby level, making articles for their own use or as gifts, perhaps selling the occasional item. A few people are operating at a commercial level, employing native flora for dyes to a greater or lesser extent complemented by imported dyestuffs.

Today's dyers are keenly aware of the issues of conservation and environmental protection associated with their practices. They are largely self-regulating and obtain materials by means that minimise the impact on stocks of wild native plants. Lichens are in general only picked in small quantities in areas where they are abundant, and then often just windblown tufts are used. Concern about the chemicals used in the dyeing process has led to a significant decrease in the usage of environmentally harmful mordants, and some dyers are experimenting with a view to discovering less harmful substances for use in the dyeing process.

There is no doubt that interest in natural dyeing will continue. A significant number of consumers are keen to purchase items manufactured using natural processes. The innate enthusiasm of makers will ensure that the practice will be furthered and greater insights gained into the practices of our forebears.

Glossary

Extracted from Dalby: *Natural Dyes for Vegetable Fibres,* with some additions by the author.

ALTERANT   alkali or acid addition to dye-bath to produce variations in colour.
CUDBEAR   a commercial preparation of orchil dye.
DYE-BATH   the liquor resulting from boiling dyestuff in water in the dye pan.
FUGITIVE   a dye that will fade during the washing process or on exposure to light.
MORDANT   a substance, usually metal salt, which chemically fixes the dye to the fibre.
ORCHIL   a type of dye, obtained from some species of lichen through a fermentation process, that produces red to purple colours.
SUBSTANTIVE   a dye that is relatively fast to washing and exposure to light.

Further reading

Dalby, G: *Natural Dyes for Vegetable Fibres* (Ashgill Publications, 1992).
Fraser, J: *Traditional Scottish Dyes* (Canongate, 1983).
Grierson, S: *The Colour Cauldron* (Oliver MacPherson Ltd, Forfar, 1986).
Mairet, E: *Vegetable Dyes* (Faber and Faber, 1938).
Rice, M and Beebee, D: *Mushrooms for Color* (Mad River Press, 1980).
Thurstan, V: *The Use of Vegetable Dyes for Beginners* (Dryad Press, 1939).

Opposite and below
Checking the colour during the dyeing process.

Hand-spun woollen cloth, called 'clò mór' (the 'big cloth'), has been woven in the Western Isles, as elsewhere in the Highlands, for centuries. Clò mór was first sold to London from the Isle of Harris in the mid-nineteenth century, and it became known as Harris Tweed at this time. As demand for the cloth grew, commercial weaving spread to Lewis and the Uists. A carding mill was established in Harris in 1900, and soon afterwards carding and spinning mills were set up in both Lewis and Harris, allowing production to increase. Gradually mill-spun and dyed yarn replaced hand-spun yarn, metal Hattersley treadle looms (and more recently double-width looms, which require less effort to operate) replaced wooden hand-looms and the finishing processes were removed to the mills, but a dwindling number of weavers in Harris continued to use traditional techniques. I learnt to make hand-spun weft tweed (with mill-spun warp) from the last of these traditional weavers, Marion Campbell of Plocropol, Harris, and made a living by weaving from 1989-97.

The island sheep are sheared in July and the fleeces for hand-spinning were dyed in large (thirty-gallon) pots in the open air in late summer. The most distinctive Harris Tweed dye was crotal, *Parmelia saxatalis*, a flat grey lichen which was easily gathered by scraping it off rocks. It gives wool a rich red-brown colour. An equal quantity of lichen to wool is required and the two are layered in the pot, covered with water and boiled fast for at least eight hours. Next day, the crotal can be shaken out of the fleeces, which are then washed well (most easily in a fast-flowing stream) and hung out to dry. The unique smell of crotal lingers on the wool (and cloth) for years. When hand-dyeing for tweed-making was common, crotal became scarce in some districts of the island, but it re-grows relatively quickly and is now plentiful.

Blue was obtained from indigo (an imported natural dye) by dissolving the dyestuff in de-oxygenated alkaline water and dipping the wool into the dye-bath. It comes out of the dye-bath yellow and turns blue on exposure to air; the wool is dipped into the dye and exposed to the air alternately until the desired depth of blue is obtained. Many plants give yellows and soft greens; I used ragwort flowers or ling heather tips just

Anne Campbell

Previous page
The late Marion Campbell of Plocropol,
Isle of Harris.

Opposite right
Katie Campbell weaving Harris Tweed.

Opposite left
Joan MacLennan weaving at her hand
loom.

before flowering for bright yellows, and the young tips of nettles or bracken for grey-green, using alum as the mordant for each. As I dyed large quantities at once and even colour was not important (as the colours would all be blended together later), I boiled the plant material, wool and the mordant together for an hour or two. Peat soot gives an ochre colour with unmordanted wool. A bright green can be obtained by over-dyeing an indigo with a heather dye (or vice versa). Reds, purples, oranges, and so on, can all be derived from native plants, but as large quantities of dyed wool are needed for Harris Tweed I used only common flowers, weeds and lichens, and did not experiment with rarer plants.

Below
Harris Tweed is often sold direct from
the weaver's workshop.

After dyeing, the fleeces must be teased out by hand to remove bits of plant material, then carded to blend all the colours together and arrange the fibres evenly, ready for spinning. Hand-carding is a very slow process, so it was mechanised in the early days of the industry and takes place in tweed mills. There are now only three Harris Tweed mills, all in Lewis, and only one of these, Donald Macleod (Carloway) Ltd, was able to card for hand-spinners at the time that I made tweed. About 100 pounds of wool was sent for carding at one time; this was then hand-spun using a traditional spinning wheel and used for the weft ('cross-ways' threads of the tweed). Hand-spinning is time-consuming but gives the finished cloth a uniquely soft texture.

Hand-spinning for the warp (the 'lengthways' threads of the cloth, which must be tightly-spun for strength) stopped in the 1940s or 1950s. I bought in warp yarn from the tweed mills. Warping is the process of arranging the warp colours in the desired order and is carried out by winding the threads around the stakes of a warping frame, then carefully transferring them to the warp beam of the loom and threading them through the loom heddles in the correct order.

I wove on a wooden beam loom with a flying shuttle, the 'beart mhór' (large loom), so called to distinguish it from the 'beart bheag' (small loom) which had a hand-thrown shuttle. The beart mhór was introduced to the islands at the turn of the century and was itself superseded by the metal Hattersley treadle loom in the 1920s and 1930s (and by the Bonas Griffiths double-width loom in the 1990s). The wooden loom is more suited to weaving with delicate hand-spun weft yarn. It has four foot pedals and a shuttle which is thrown across the loom by a mechanism of rollers, string and leather, operated by one hand. The other hand pulls the lay backwards and forwards, tightening the cloth as it is woven. Both feet are used on the pedals to raise and lower the heddles, forming the pattern. Good co-ordination between hands, feet and eye is needed to form an even weave.

When the tweed is removed from the loom, it is oily (with natural oil from the fleece and oil added during carding) and feels tough and stiff. To clean, soften and shrink it, it is waulked: first the tweed is washed in hot soapy water, then, while still wet and soapy, pounded by hand on a roughened wooden board for several hours, until it has shrunk in width from approximately thirty-three to twenty-nine inches. This process, along with the use of hand-spun yarn, gives this type of tweed a uniquely dense, soft finish. In the past waulkings were social occasions, when the women of the district would gather to pound the cloth on the board in keeping with the rhythm of their songs; a vast store of Gaelic songs was preserved in this way. After waulking, the tweed would be blessed before being handed over to its owner.

Each twenty-yard length of hand-spun weft tweed takes about a month to produce and is unique. This makes it difficult to market alongside modern Harris Tweed which is produced in a fraction of the time and so sells at a much lower price. I found that the only feasible way of making a living from this type of weaving was by having an 'open workshop' with demonstrations, selling directly to visitors and by mail order to contacts made via the workshop. This was a much more successful marketing strategy than trying to sell through shops and galleries, or to designers and tailors: if people do not understand the processes involved, it is difficult to justify the cost (especially as Harris Tweed is already marketed as a hand-made product). However, there was a lot of interest in hand-spun weft tweed and especially in hand-dyeing, and I managed to sell each year's production despite doing very little advertising. There is currently no one making hand-spun weft Harris Tweed but it still has potential as a viable way of making a living, especially if combined with running workshops on traditional textile skills.

Below
Wooden shuttles carry the weft threads across the loom during the weaving process.

Further reading

Thompson, F: *Harris Tweed. The Story of a Hebridean Industry* (David & Charles, Newton Abbot, 1969).

Perhaps more than any other textile in the world, tartan is surrounded by mystique and tradition. This has emerged as a consequence of events following the Jacobite Rising of 1745. Tartan the textile is possibly second only to denim cloth in its popularity and use. It has spread far beyond the textile confines of its Celtic origins. Today we can find tartan woven, printed, painted or etched, and in many other mediums. Its ubiquitous use shows tartan has indeed come a very long way from its roots.

Mention tartan and most people would immediately think of Scotland, kilts and bagpipes, but where did it come from and when? It is certainly true that Scotland has a strong claim to a place in the history of tartan. The development of tartan reached its height in Scotland with the nineteenth-century concept of clan tartans. Indeed it could be argued that it is still developing, with new tartans being designed almost daily by a successful international industry. However, tartan's pedigree is far older than its use in Scotland. The tartan pattern seems to have developed in parallel with the use of wool for textiles. It came to Scotland with the Celtic peoples whose movement from the Caucasus, westward, eventually spread to this far fringe of Europe. Here they left their language, which developed into Gaelic, and their textile – tartan.

Relatively little is known about tartan before 1700. Due to the acidic nature of much of the Highland soil very few fragments of cloth survive and information about tartan is generally found in travellers' tales or other documents. From Roman times until the Renaissance, writers referred to the Highlanders as wearing striped cloaks of many colours. After the failure of the last Jacobite Rising in 1746, the kilt and tartan were banned in an attempt to stamp out the culture seen by the Hanoverian government as the power base of the Stewart kings. The ban, imposed by Act of Parliament of 1746, forbade men and boys to 'wear or put on Highland clothes including the kilt, plaid and no tartan or party-coloured plaid or stuff was to be used for Great Coats or for Upper Coats'. The Act did not apply to those men serving as soldiers in Highland Regiments, or to gentry, the sons of gentry, or women. The proscription of Highland dress lasted for a period of thirty-six years before being repealed in 1782, by which time much of the

TARTAN, A WORLD CLASS TEXTILE

Peter MacDonald

old lore and skills of tartan manufacture had been lost or discarded as inappropriate to the new politico-economic circumstances in which the Highlanders found themselves. However, under the Act, the ban only affected 'that part of North Britain called Scotland'; the area north of a line from Dumbarton in the west to Perth in the east. The direct result of this was that tartan production moved from the Highlands to south of the Highland line where the firm of William Wilson & Son developed in Bannockburn near Stirling. For over 150 years this firm was to dominate the development of tartan in Scotland. Indeed most, if not all, of the pre-1850 patterns bearing clan, regimental or district names can be traced to Wilsons.

Traditional dyestuffs

It is easy to picture a time when a Highland family collected various berries, barks, flowers and lichens from their local area with which to dye the wool that they had spun from their own sheep. While this may once have been true, in reality imported dyes have probably been a feature of tartan since they were first introduced, particularly from about 1600. It was around the turn of the seventeenth century that the two great dyestuffs, indigo and cochineal, first appeared in Scotland. These were to have a dramatic effect on the type of pattern that could be woven. Although the generic colours given by these dyes, blue and red respectively, were available from indigenous plants, the shades tended to be paler, duller and generally less fast. It is likely that a tartan containing a large amount of red would not have been usual before the introduction of cochineal, but this dye, together with indigo, gave dyers access to deep reds, blues, purples and greens previously unknown in Scottish tartans. What a change from the dull greens, yellows and browns, perhaps with blue or pink stripes, the imported dyes must have made. Although a good blue was available from indigenous woad, this plant was more difficult to use in that it required greater amounts of dyestuff and even then the result was never as dark as with indigo. However, it was cochineal that was really to change things. This dye held sway until the mid-1800s when the first aniline or

Below
The pleats of the kilt are steam pressed
into place on this McDonald tartan.

chemical dyes were introduced. To own something dyed with cochineal was a status symbol until well into the nineteenth century. It is interesting to look at portraits of Highland chiefs before about 1850. In a majority of these red features as a dominant colour; by wearing it the chief was making a social statement. A parallel can be drawn with the use of purple by the Romans for the togas of the rich and famous.

The need for mass-production of cloth to meet large orders, such as those from the military, led to a requirement for standard colours and patterns in order to maintain quality control. These standardised colours and patterns were devised by Wilsons of Bannockburn and were in use by them by the 1780s. Their range continued to grow with the increase in the demand for tartan; a trend that continued throughout the nineteenth century. By the time the first aniline dye was introduced in 1856 the use of standard patterns, colours and colour terminology had been practised by Wilsons for over seventy years and was firmly established. The concept of standardisation has been developed by the weaving companies of today into a set of standard ranges such as Old, Modern and Muted colours.

Hand-weaving

Until the 'industrial revolution' all weaving, and related processes such as spinning, was done by hand. At one time there were estimated to be 78,000 hand-weavers in Scotland, although only a relatively small proportion of these would have been weaving tartan. With the advent of industrial production the weavers were initially drawn together to work in a common locality while still using their own loom. Soon entrepreneurs began to provide new, modern looms under a single roof. As mechanised looms developed, so weavers began to specialise in the shuttle work (throwing the shuttle and beating the cloth). Increased mechanisation resulted in today's full automation, where a loom worker will have responsibility for several power looms but not for the actual weaving. In reality they are now plant-operators and no longer weavers.

Hand-weaving is still practised commercially by a few people, although none are thought to work exclusively on tartan any longer. Unfortunately the time required to produce a length of cloth by hand means that it is difficult to make a living in modern Britain solely by weaving, although the art will undoubtedly live on as a hobby. The differences between a hand-woven and machine-woven piece of cloth are difficult to describe. Most people will never have seen hand-woven tartan, nor are they likely ever to own a piece. The qualities of good hand-woven cloth, as revealed by the way it drapes and hangs, the so-called 'handle', have been replaced by the smoother and stiffer machine-woven cloth, arguably to the detriment of pattern.

Tartan patterns

Wilsons of Bannockburn started to name some of their patterns after towns and districts in the latter half of the eighteenth century. Early in the nineteenth century the use of family names for tartans begins to predominate and this practice increased over the next fifty years.

Wilsons appear to have collected a number of old patterns from the Highlands and produced variations of them for a tartan-hungry public. The naming of clan and family patterns was given a huge boost by George IV's Royal Visit to Edinburgh in 1822. He was the first king to visit Scotland for 150 years and the event was, to a large degree, stage managed by Sir Walter Scott who urged the Scots to turn out 'plaided and plumed' in their true tartans to meet their King. This led James Logan to complain in his 1831 book *The Scottish Gael* that this appeal had 'combined to excite much curiosity among all classes, to ascertain the particular tartans and badges they were entitled to wear. This creditable feeling undoubtedly led to a result different from what might have been expected: fanciful varieties of tartan and badges were passed off as genuine.'

The practice of designing new patterns continued during the nineteenth and early twentieth centuries and in recent years has outstripped even the ability of Wilsons to produce new patterns. Three developments have made this possible. First and foremost has been the continual technical innovation that has allowed production to meet demand. Coupled very closely to this has been the advertising and commercial promotion of tartan by the manufacturers and fashion industry. Finally, the widespread and increasing availability of computers with design programmes during the past ten years has led to anyone with a Scottish or tartan interest being able to have a go at designing their own tartan. The combination of the fashion market and the ability of individuals to design their own tartan has probably been the biggest change in the development of tartan since the mass production of the early nineteenth century. This change reflects a move away from the traditional design techniques common to earlier innovations. The use and combination of colours and shades that would not have been considered appropriate in traditional tartans has expanded the market potential for tartan. So, for example, a blue, green and red tartan might go down well in Scotland or Italy, but in Asia something with scarlet, yellow, purple and orange might be preferred.

Today tartan, whether hand or machine woven, will use machine-spun yarn often produced from imported wool. The dyes too are nowadays all chemical, although they attempt to recreate the original natural dyes. To set up a hand-loom for traditional width (twenty-eight inch) tartan cloth takes about a day. Thereafter the cloth can be hand-woven at a rate ranging from one to six yards per day depending on the type of loom, the complexity of the design and the skill of the weaver. Using machine-spun and dyed yarn, a kilt length can be completed in about three days. If the whole process is done by hand, the equivalent length would take about three weeks. Compare this with about four hours for a fully automated length of cloth and it is easy to understand why the hand-weaver has become an endangered species. Given the time involved to produce a piece of cloth it can be appreciated that such cloth is now mostly woven on a commission basis with the client often being from the so-called Scottish diaspora: those of Scottish descent now living overseas.

Until tartan was banned in 1747 there may have
been as few as 100 tartans in existence. Today
there are at least 3500 and new ones are
designed almost daily. This makes the recording
and authenticating work extremely difficult for
the two bodies concerned with Scotland's tartan
heritage: the Scottish Tartans Authority and the
Scottish Tartans Society.

Tartan, once simply a rural, cultural art form, is
now found in many areas of daily life from the
traditional kilt of Scotland to the international
world of corporate business. The enduring
romantic and heroic overtones surrounding
tartan means one can understand its use by the
Bank of Scotland and even British Airways, but
what about *Encyclopaedia Britannica*, the Cree
Indian Nation, or the FBI?

Over the last fifty years or so tartan has
developed into a multi-million pound industry
dominated by a few large Scottish mills. Its
appeal is truly international – a success story
that could have never been imagined in those
dark days of 1747-82 when its use was banned.
Today tartan holds a unique place in the annals
of textile history and has come to symbolise,
along with the kilt and bagpipes, the cultural
identity of the whole Scottish nation.

Glossary

BEATING THE CLOTH	after the shuttle carrying the weft thread is thrown across the warp the thread is packed tight using the beater.
DENT	The spaces in a reed through which the yarn is passed; the whole reed then acts as a comb and beater to pack the yarn tight.
EPI ENDS PER INCH	the number or density of warp threads to the inch.
ELL	an old unit of measurement, the Scotch ell was thirty-seven inches, the standard reed length by the time of the *1819 Key Pattern Book*.
HERRINGBONE	a technique often found on the selvage of old specimens of tartan: the twill weave is reversed back and forth in bands of commonly ten threads making a form of overlocking.
HESP	a unit of measurement used in dyeing: 1800 yards, made up of six haers.
OFFSET	the old practice of measuring a warp from the centre of one pivot to the selvage mark on the other. When put onto the loom the warp then appears unbalanced compared with the contemporary practice of measuring a pattern equally from the centre to give a balanced warp. The old offset patterns were made either for joining to form a wide plaid, or for kilt cloth with a selvage mark.
PLAID	(pronounced 'plad' not 'played'), derives from the Gaelic word 'plaide' meaning 'blanket'. In North America the term is widely used in place of 'tartan' when referring to checked patterns.
PLAIN WEAVE	a weave where each thread passes alternately under one thread going in the opposite direction and then over the next, and so on.
PORTER	twenty splits or dents in a reed. So, in the 24 reed: 24 porters x 37 inches = 888 dents.
SELVAGE	sometimes selvedge, literally the self-edge where the crossing weft threads are bound around the outer warp ones creating a non-fraying edge.
SELVAGE MARK	a band of colour or colours extended to the edge of the cloth above the thread-count for the particular colour. Military selvage marks were solid black while civilian ones often comprised bands of two or more colours.
SETT	the arrangement of the different colours making up the pattern.
SYND	to wash lightly, to prepare yarn by soaking, to rinse.
THROWING THE SHUTTLE	the process of passing the shuttle, between the warp threads, from one side of the loom to the other
TWILL WEAVE	usually tartan is woven as a 2/2 twill where each thread goes alternately over two then under two threads going in the opposite direction. Each successive thread begins one place later, resulting in the classic staggered effect of this weave.

Below

Selection of pieces: Caledonia, Gordon and Young.

Further reading

Campbell, A: *Campbell Tartan* (Beinn Bhuidhe Holdings Ltd, Inverary, 1985).

Cheape, H: *Tartan. The Highland Habit* (National Museums of Scotland, Edinburgh, 1991), second edition, 1995.

Dunbar, J T: *The History of Highland Dress* (Oliver & Boyd, Edinburgh, 1962).

Grierson, S: *The Colour Cauldron* (Oliver McPherson Ltd, Forfar, 1986).

Grant, N: *Scottish Clans & Tartans* (Hamlyn, London, 1987).

Hesketh, C: *Tartans* (Octopus Books, London, 1972).

Liles, J N: *The Art and Craft of Natural Dyeing* (University of Tennessee Press, Knoxville, 1990).

Logan, J: *The Scottish Gael* (Smith, Eldar & Co, London, 1831).

Logan, J and R R McIan: *The Clans of the Scottish Highlands* (Ackermann & Co, London, 1845).

MacDonald, M: *The Clans of Scotland* (Brian Todd Publishing Ltd, London, 1991).

MacDonald, P: *The 1819 Key Pattern Book – One Hundred Original Tartans* (Jamieson & Munro, Perth, 1996).

Martine, R: *Scottish Clan and Family Names* (John Bartholomew & Son Ltd, Edinburgh, 1987).

Munro, R W: *Highland Clans & Tartans* (Octopus Books, London, 1977).

Scarlett, J D: *The Tartan-Spotter's Guide* (Shepheard-Walwyn, London, 1973).

Scarlett, J D: *The Tartan Weaver's Guide* (Shepheard-Walwyn, London, 1985).

Scarlett, J D: *Tartan: The Highland Textile* (Shepheard-Walwyn, London, 1990).

Smith, W & A: *Authenticated Tartans of the Clans and Families of Scotland* (W & A Smith, Mauchline, 1850).

Stewart, D C: *The Setts of the Scottish Tartans* (Oliver & Boyd, Edinburgh 1950), revised edition (Shepheard Walwyn, London, 1977).

Stewart, D C and Thompson, J C: *Scotland's Forged Tartans* (Paul Harris Publishing, Edinburgh, 1980).

Teall of Teallach, D G and P D Smith: *District Tartans* (Shepheard-Walwyn, London, 1992).

Addresses

SCOTTISH TARTANS AUTHORITY

Dept STA
51 Atholl Street
Pitlochry
Perthshire PH16 5BU

SCOTTISH TARTANS SOCIETY

Hall of Records
Fonab
Pitlochry
Perthshire PH16

Arthur Edmondston MD wrote in 1808: 'The manufactures of Zetland are but few, but the knitting of worsted stockings, caps and gloves, on wires, by the women, is amongst the most ancient.' Hand-knitting has played an important role in the economic, social and aesthetic history of Shetland. It is a human story, which started in the ninth century or earlier, and remains tenuously with us today. In the past the income from hand-knitting supplemented a basic economy of subsistence crofting. The men went to sea; the women stayed at home, worked the croft and knitted. The Shetland economy was traditionally based on fishing, crofting and knitting, yet hand-knitting has always been undervalued and unrecorded. Knitting was regarded as women's work of low commercial value, echoing their traditionally low status in society.

The knitters' unorganised labour force had little bargaining power. Knitters dealt through merchant shopkeepers who bound them to a 'truck system', which forced them to take payment in goods from the shop, instead of money. The Royal Commissioners on the truck system visited Shetland in 1872, and their findings provide the single most informed account of the social and economic conditions of Shetland women in the nineteenth century. The document is an indictment of exploitation and fraud, a situation the women had accepted with resignation. The system, although illegal, continued until the 1940s when the armed forces stationed in Shetland bought knitwear for cash from the knitters, and thus ended it for ever.

During the 1920s and 1930s there were serious attempts to organise the hand-knitting industry and to impose quality control. By the 1950s knitting machines were in general use, often operated by men. The women continued to hand-knit the Fair Isle yokes and borders of the garments. The oil era of the 1970s brought about social and economic changes, which had a devastating and permanent effect on the hand-knitting industry. Modern technology replaced the knitters who had left the industry for more lucrative oil-related work, never to return.

In 1982 the Shetland Islands Council, determined not to lose Shetland's traditional industries to the all-engulfing oil industry, founded the Shetland Knitwear Trades

SHETLAND AND FAIR ISLE KNITTING

Margaret Stuart

Association (SKTA), funded by oil revenues, to promote and protect real Shetland knitwear. The SKTA embarked on an impressive programme of promotional events, supported by professional fashion photography. Stands were taken at international trade fairs, where members could show their own collections and take orders.

Shetland lace and Fair Isle knitwear

Lace knitting became the mainstay of the Shetland knitwear industry in the latter half of the nineteenth century. The industry had been in decline, but recovered with the introduction of the finer and more specialised items so beloved by the Victorians, such as elaborately patterned shawls, lace stockings, mitts, veils, gloves and soft warm underclothing. Queen Victoria was presented with fine lace stockings; and Edward Standen, a hosiery merchant from Oxford, commissioned an elaborate lace shawl for the Great Exhibition of 1851. Shetland lace enjoyed royal patronage and gifts of fine lace were presented to royalty on special occasions such as a royal marriage. Crowns, initials and dates were often included in the design. Fine lace shawls and scarves continued to be knitted in the first half of the twentieth century and lacy jumpers became fashionable in the 1930s and 1940s.

The craft of two-coloured stranded knitting was known throughout northern Europe by the seventeenth century. The demand for plain knitted garments took preference over patterned knitting, but by 1850 the knitters on Fair Isle had become known for their brightly coloured, richly patterned knitwear, which they traded with visitors and passing ships, often rowing out a great distance to barter their goods. In 1814 Sir Walter Scott visited the island, and wrote to his wife, 'the women of Fair Isle knit stockings and a queer kind of night cap and mitts. I have bought some, but they must be well scoured'.

At the beginning of the twentieth century the fall in demand for plain knitwear coincided with the rise in popularity of patterned knitwear. Knitters on mainland Shetland were quick to see the potential and Fair Isle patterns were passed from knitter to knitter, much to the indignation of those on Fair Isle.

Above
Scarf, hand-knitted on Fair Isle *c*.1880. The wool is hand-spun and hand-dyed. Natural black and white from native sheep, yellow from lichen, and red and blue from madder and indigo imported into Fair Isle and sold in the shop.

In 1922 the Prince of Wales wore a Fair Isle pullover as Captain of the Royal and Ancient Golf Club at St Andrews. With this royal seal of approval, Fair Isle knitwear gained popularity. The exuberance of colour and patterns symbolised the Jazz Age and Fair Isle pullovers were soon worn in fashionable circles from the golf course to the ski slope.

No creative craft stands still, and during the next forty years knitters experimented with colour from commercial home dyes, and with artificial silk and rayon thread. Some knitters abandoned the horizontal bands of pattern for trellis and vertical panel patterned garments, and Norwegian star patterns were adapted to complement every garment. The Fair Isle yoke sweater became the trademark of the 1950s. There was a revival in the 1970s of the traditional patterns and colours of the nineteenth century, and the first designer knits made their appearance.

Shetland is the last region where crafts-people continue to practise the regional variation of their craft, hand-knitting, on a commercial scale. The reason for this phenomenon is the character of the older, and last, generation of commercial hand-knitters, who cannot sit 'haand idle'. They have knitted since childhood, and knitting needles and knitting belt have become an integral part of their lives. Good hand-knitters willing to knit allover Fair Isle garments are in great demand, and courted by the knitwear manufacturers. Wool and patterns are delivered to the knitter, and completed garments collected and dressed. The production of hand-knitted allover Fair Isle garments is very limited, and customers are advised to treasure their purchase. The knitters use traditional patterns, because they are familiar and can be knitted at great speed. Most hand-knitters concentrate on accessories in Fair Isle and lace, often to complement machine-made garments, using the same patterns and colour schemes.

As the number of hand-knitters and hand-frame machine-knitters declines, manufacturers are relying more and more on computer-operated machines. The Shetland knitwear industry is based on 500 years of unique tradition and enjoys an international reputation. Manufacturers are aware of this and continue to use the

Above
Fair Isle knitting c.1925. Tortoiseshell knitting needles and 'makkin' belt – worn around the waist with the pad (horsehair) to the left. One knitting needle is firmly inserted into the pad to increase speed and evenness of knitting. 'Makkin' belts are still used by knitters in Shetland today.

Below
This detail shows Norwegian influence
in the vertical panel design.

distinctive Fair Isle patterns. Japan has become the largest and most consistent importer of Shetland knitwear, from small orders for allover Fair Isle hand-knit garments, to enormous orders for thousands of machine-made garments. The 'Scottish style' is very popular in Japan and customers regard it as important to have the 'real thing'. Prestigious exhibitions and well-researched media coverage in Japan have created an image of remote and windswept islands, steeped in history, the perfect background for timeless garments. The sale of hand-knitted accessories from Shetland to Italy and France also remains constant, and the home market is growing steadily, as more and more people recognise the quality product on their doorstep.

Fair Isle Co-operative

In 1980 Fair Isle Crafts Ltd Co-operative was launched and, some years later, a distinctive HAND-FRAME KNITTED trademark was registered. The islanders agreed that to take full advantage of their unique position as the source of Fair Isle patterned knitting in Shetland, they would have to maximise production and price. In order to produce the quantity of knitwear to make the project viable, the Co-op decided to use hand-frame machines to knit allover Fair Isle garments. The knitwear is displayed and sold in the community hall and order books are full.

Local trade and tourist market

The four largest knitwear manufacturers have shops in Lerwick, the capital town of Shetland, selling knitwear directly to the public. Most of their production of hand-knitted garments and accessories sells from the shop, because production is piecemeal and cannot be relied upon to fulfil orders. Local shops stock up during the winter months when most of the knitting is done, ready for the tourist season, a trade bolstered by the huge cruise liners that call regularly during the summer months, disgorging hundreds of passengers for a few hours shopping in the town.

There are several venues in the town where visitors can see demonstrations of hand-spinning and hand-knitting, Fair Isle and lace, and purchase hand-knitted garments and lace shawls directly from the knitters. During the summer the local agricultural shows encourage small knitwear manufacturers to take stalls to sell their products. Across mainland Shetland and the Isles, visitors can buy garments direct from the factories at mill prices, or order hand-knitted, personally-designed garments from individuals who offer 'Knitwear for Sale' at their houses.

Residential and day courses in hand-spinning, dyeing and hand-knitting are available to visitors seeking a more rewarding holiday experience. Many visitors come to Shetland expressly to learn to spin and knit. There is no comparison in feel and warmth between a garment hand-knitted from hand-spun wool and one knitted from machine-spun wool. In the past the spinning wheel was closely integrated into the life of Shetland women, every item of clothing and bedding was knitted or woven from hand-spun thread. Once a necessity, spinning now fulfills a desire in people to acquire a knowledge of how something as fundamental as cloth is made from raw wool.

Shows, events and competitions

Competitions in local and national shows can be a great incentive and challenge to crafts people. The Royal Highland Show (RHS) Handcrafts Competition has a strong textile section and a group of spinners and knitters from Shetland regularly compete with considerable success. The number of entries for Fair Isle and lace knitting at the RHS is increasing annually, while entries in the agricultural shows in Shetland is decreasing.

The Scottish Women's Rural Institutes (SWRI) in Shetland have always had a special role in the preservation and contemporary application of the traditional skills of spinning and hand-knitting Fair Isle and lace. The Federation of the SWRI holds a bi-annual exhibition/competition in the historic Town Hall in Lerwick. The standard of work and display is extremely high and a large section is devoted to textile crafts.

Below
Ann Eunson spinning fine wool
yarn in Shetland.

Demonstrations of spinning and knitting are an effective way of raising public appreciation of craft-skills and an understanding of the value of the finished article. Textile crafts are particularly suitable for demonstration. Spinning wheels, small looms and needles are easy to transport. It is not a problem in Shetland to bring together a group of spinners and knitters to demonstrate their skills and, at most public events, shows, and village hall teas, visitors are encouraged to 'have a go'.

The Shetland Guild of Spinners, Weavers and Dyers and the Weisdale Mill

The Shetland Guild of Spinners, Weavers and Dyers was formed in 1988 with the aim of preserving and extending the knowledge of the traditional textile skills of Shetland. Today an enthusiastic group meets monthly at different locations in Shetland for lectures, workshops, demonstrations and a social. Ideas, skills and information are exchanged and visitors are welcome to join the group.

The historic Weisdale Mill houses the Shetland Textile Working Museum, an independent enterprise run by the Guild, which has become a focus for textiles in Shetland. The basement floor of the mill is leased to the Guild by the Shetland Arts Trust. The area is used to house the Guild's museum collection of historic Shetland knitwear, artefacts and ephemera. It also provides office and workshop space, and Guild members have organised several successful workshops in spinning and hand-knitting for groups from home and abroad. Each year the Guild's summer exhibition explores a different aspect of Shetland's textile heritage.

Background photograph, opposite
Knitting is taught to all primary school children in Shetland.

Opposite left
Fleece, carders ('cairds') and spools.

Opposite right
Balls of hand-spun wool.

The Shetland Education Department shows great vision in its policy of teaching knitting to all primary school children in Shetland. The schools are divided between fourteen dedicated instructors and each year the Guild hosts an exhibition of 'Bairns' Wark' (children's work) at the Weisdale Mill. The Shetland College Textile Department offers a two-year Textile Course leading to a Diploma in Higher Education and entry to a degree course in textiles at an art college on mainland Britain, a far cry from the low status

Below
Fair Isle-pattern knitting, 1910, with bone
needles and 'makkin wisps'. The pointed
end of the wisp was tucked into the
knitter's belt or waistband and one
needle was placed into it to support the
knitting in progress. This increased the
speed and evenness of the work. Old
wisps, such as these, were made from
bundles of feather quills bound together
with braid.

accorded to knitters in the past. On application, the Textile Department will arrange a course for a student, or group of students, in hand-knitting Fair Isle and Shetland lace.

Other textile forms in Shetland

The Norse settlers of the ninth century brought their native sheep with them; the wool was woven into 'wadmal', a coarse cloth. Cloth continued to be woven by the crofter in the home, for family use, until the end of the nineteenth century. Some merchants expanded their business into weaving, giving out spun wool to be woven into cloth by the crofters in their homes. Later, looms were installed in weaving-sheds around Shetland to create a more organised working environment. The last hand-weaver ceased work in 1996.

In 1993 Jamieson's Spinning Mill bought a disused knitwear factory at Sandness and installed industrial looms to produce double-width Shetland Tweed from their own wool. Shetland Tweed has special qualities – it is lightweight and fine textured, yet warm; the colours are both subtle and suddenly dazzling. Most of the production is exported to Japan.

'Taatit rugs' are peculiar to Shetland, although similar to rugs made in Norway. They were originally made as bed rugs. It is recorded that during the eighteenth century 'taatit rugs' were sold to foreign seamen in Lerwick. The rug 'grund' (ground) is made from coarsely woven wool, the 'taats' are looped over two fingers and secured to the grund with a needle, and cut to make a shaggy pile.

There has been a recent revival of interest in Shetland rug-making; a member of the Guild, having made a Shetland 'taatit' rug herself, gave a workshop, and so passed on a near forgotten skill.

Opposite
Detail of beret knitted on Fair Isle
c.1860. Natural brown and white, yellow
dyed with lichen, and red and blue from
imported madder and indigo.

Below

Fair Isle patterned hand-knitting
c.1940 (detail).

Below

Fair Isle patterned hand-knitting
c.1940 (detail).

Conclusion

The Shetland Knitwear Industry is now in the hands of three large companies in Shetland, one of whom, Jamieson's Spinning, has a spinning mill, a Shetland knitwear factory, a Shetland Tweed mill, and a shop in town. A few small knitwear producers are providing work for the last generation of hand-knitters and hand-frame knitters, who are probably doing what they most enjoy. The large companies have planned their knitwear production for the future based on machines, not people, but still retaining that continuous thread of tradition that has remained unbroken for 500 years.

I would like to pay tribute to the countless unacclaimed hand-knitters of the past, who through their skill and fortitude laid the foundations of the present knitwear industry. They knitted far into the night, and as they walked to and from their daily tasks, for a meagre return, resigned to the injustices of life.

Glossary

GARMENTS DRESSED	all knitwear in Shetland is washed and put on an appropriate shaped wooden frame to dry.
GRUND	woven wool ground for rugs.
HAAND IDLE	hand idle, doing nothing.
MAKKIN'	making
MAKKIN' WISP	a bound bundle of feather quills into which one needle is inserted during the knitting process.
TAAT	thick worsted yarn for making rugs.
TAATIT rug	originally used as bed rugs. The 'taats' are cut to give a shaggy pile to the rug.
WIRES	steel knitting needles.

Further reading

Fenton, *A: The Northern Isles. Orkney and Shetland* (John Donald Publishers, Edinburgh, 1978).
Fryer, L G: *Knitting by the Fireside and on the Hillside* (*The Shetland Times*, Shetland, 1995).
Graham, J J: *The Shetland Dictionary* (*The Shetland Times*, Shetland, 1993).
Nicolson, J R: *Traditional Life in Shetland* (Lowe & Brydone, Norfolk, 1978).
Rutt, Richard: *A History of Hand Knitting* (Batsford, London, 1987).
Thom, V M: *Fair Isle. An Island Saga* (John Donald, Edinburgh, 1989).

Opposite

Toggles, buttons and zips.

One of the most distinctive furniture types anywhere in Europe is the Orkney Chair. Its vertical wooden frame and curving straw back are instantly recognisable and replicated nowhere else – with one exception: on Fair Isle, the most southerly of the Shetland Islands. The Orkney and Fair Isle traditions are distinct, however, on account of the methods used to make the backs. Straw chairs were, at one time, common throughout those parts of Britain and Ireland, including Wales, the English West Country and East Anglia, where straw-working was commonly practised. Today, although wicker chairs are still made in England, the production of straw-backed chairs is confined to the far north of Scotland.

In Orkney, because of the strong winter winds, there are few trees and for countless centuries straw and stone often took the place of timber. Driftwood was too precious and imported timber too expensive to be made into furniture when straw was a satisfactory substitute. What timber existed was needed for boats, ploughs and those parts of the house not made from stone and straw, such as roof couples. The earliest Orkney Chairs to survive today were made almost entirely of straw with only thin strips of wood to provide a framework. They were essentially inverted baskets with a curved straw back, and for every chair of this kind there were probably a dozen straw stools.

Orcadians were adept at using straw, primarily for baskets (kaesies, cubbies, luppies), but also for mats (flackies), as bedding, and even for shoes. Simmens, or straw ropes, were used to roof houses, the thickly laced ropes forming the base for a layer of turf and thatch held down by more ropes. At one time even straw was too valuable as fodder to be used in such large quantities and simmens were made from heather. Even where flagstone was used as roofing, straw simmens were laid over as insulation.

The form recognisable today as the Orkney Chair is little more than 150 years old and has probably survived thanks only to the entrepreneurial efforts of the Kirkwall joiner David Munro Kirkness. Kirkness was born in 1854 on Westray and began to make Orkney Chair frames in about 1878. He had the backs woven by outworkers, either

Stephen Jackson

Below
Stewart Thomson of Fair Isle carving
the arm of his chair.

crofters working in the evenings or fishermen at times ashore. The half-timbered form that he used, however, had been developed several decades previously. Surviving examples of these early chairs are generally boxed-in around the legs, with or without a drawer, draught-resistance being a central feature of the design.

Kirkness' success derived from his ability to market the chairs on the Scottish mainland. He adapted the form to suit the market for arts and crafts furniture, being the first to replace plain boarded seats with woven sea-grass ones and boxed-in legs with an open framework. He died in 1936, having supplied chairs to the Royal Family and to major furniture retailers throughout the Empire. The business was carried on until 1978. Throughout the twentieth century there continued to be people, particularly on the outer islands such as Westray, Sanday and Eday, who made the occasional chair for friends and family. Today the production of the chairs is divided between those for whom it is a business, employing a limited number of assistants or outworkers, and those for whom the work is a supplementary form of income.

The making of the straw chair back is a time-consuming task and every maker follows a slightly different pattern. Today the timber frame is assembled, with or without a drawer below the seat, from imported oak or, less commonly, from driftwood. In prehistoric times the only wood to be used in either Orkney or Shetland was washed ashore from the virgin forests of North America, although by the Middle Ages the wealthy imported timber from Scandinavia and the Baltic. The best straw for chair and basket-work comes from black Murkle oats. An inferior grain that nevertheless thrives on poor soils and can withstand strong winds and heavy rain, it is grown in only the smallest quantities today for its thin, supple and robust straw. This is harvested in September or October and stacked over the winter (tied down with simmens).

When ready for use, the grain is simply cut off and the straw dressed, that is the loose leaves removed by hand. Lengths of straw are bundled together and the first row nailed to the seat. New lengths of straw are added almost constantly as the work progresses

and are held in place with a metal or wooden ring that also regulates the thickness of the bundle. The back is essentially a continuous series of rows turned back upon itself at the wooden uprights and either nailed or laced with string to these uprights. As the straw is wound back and forth, the rows are sewn together using a flat-headed needle and a single length of sisal string. The last row of a standard chair is finished with tightly wound sisal. This sisal is imported, although in the past locally gathered 'bent', or sea-grass, would have been used.

Most makers today choose to make a fairly angular shaped back which draws away from the base about a quarter of the distance up. Older chairs were often more rounded in appearance. Hoods are either built up as a continuation of the back, or begun from the centre of the back in an arching pattern; with both methods the result is very similar. Any remaining rough hairs of straw can be singed off by quickly moving a flame (or blowlamp) across the surface. In all, the making of the straw back alone can take up to a week. Drop-in seats of woven sea-grass tend to be more popular than plain boarded seats. Although timber is imported, the rest of the process is remarkably sustainable, with the oat waste going to feed chickens and timber waste burnt to smoke salmon.

The Shetland Islands differ from Orkney in many respects and are generally characterised as a place where fishing and trade were more important than arable farming. While this was broadly true, straw-crafts were still well-developed and on Fair Isle, the most southerly of the Islands, straw-backed chairs were being made in the nineteenth century. They are today made only by one man, Stewart Thomson. He continues to live a crofting way of life in which agriculture, chair-making and the upkeep of an aerogenerator all contribute to his income. He grows his own Shetland oats, which yield an exceptionally long straw, and his timber is a mixture of imported hardwoods and salvaged wreck-wood. His design, which follows that used by his grandfather, Jerome Wilson, looks not unlike an Orkney Chair. The back, however, is woven with cotton string using surgeon's knots in a manner that recalls the net-

Below
Sewing in progress.

Above
Finished lacing.

Below
The Orkney Chair back is one
continuous length of straws turning back
upon itself at the wooden uprights.

making skills of fishermen. The straw is worked back and forth in a similar way to the Orkney Chair, but each row is held in place by roughly thirty-six pairs of string threads, knotted across each row. All of Stewart Thomson's chairs have boarded seats and two tapering rear uprights give added support to the straight-framed back.

At the time of writing there are about half a dozen makers of straw-backed chairs in Orkney, roughly half of whom are based in Kirkwall, the rest on outer islands. The majority are men, many of whom worked previously in other occupations including agriculture and fishing. A few are women, however, in an economy in which employment opportunities for women are scarce. For some of these islanders chair-making provides an additional source of income, as it did for their grandfathers, and even on islands where no chairs are produced commercially there are residents who make the occasional piece. Although some makers are now in their seventies or eighties, the techniques are being handed down to a new generation, ready to market their chairs globally via the internet. A significant proportion of their work is sold to American and continental European clients and the prospects for the Scottish straw-backed chair are bright.

Opposite
Stewart Thomson, chairmaker,
outside his home, Fair Isle.

The transition from sail and oar power to the use of steam and the internal combustion engine is a significant waypoint in the course of traditional boat-building in Scotland. Wooden boats had evolved to achieve the very best from the union of man's ingenuity with the natural elements of wood, wind and water. Scottish fishing boats through the centuries embodied the principles of Viking ships, but suitably adapted to match local conditions and resources. So when sail eventually gave way to steam and oil, it was quite simply a matter of applying this new technology to existing boats; and for many years to follow, even into the late 1950s, it was common to see a combination of both sail and engine power. In some cases the engine was only needed to help in the event of insufficient wind.

It was in 1960 that the White Fish Authority issued a 'Standard Specification for the Construction of Scottish Wooden Fishing Vessels' for motor boats between thirty feet and ninety feet in length, as a minimum standard towards grant and loan eligibility. Several excellent motor fishing-boat designs emerged as a result, and a great many were built in various boatyards around the Scottish coast and islands during the next twenty years or so: drifters, trawlers, ringers and seine-netters.

Electronic fishing aids and more sophisticated catching methods dramatically increased earning power and consequently even bigger boats with greater potential were built in steel and glass-reinforced plastic, materials which were very soon to dominate the boat-building scene. This trend, coupled with stringent legislation on catching capacity, has all but eliminated the once vibrant wooden boat-building industry.

The phenomenal upsurge in marine leisure activity during this period has resulted in large-scale production practices being applied to the fabrication of sports and pleasure boats ranging from canoes and kayaks up to multi-hulled ocean-racing machines. Modern technology has brought the one-time exclusive pursuits of the elite yachting world within easy reach of many. Consequently, many long-established yacht-builders have been forced to give way to 'off the shelf' market forces, or, as some have done, adapt to the new methods.

COASTAL AND ISLAND BOATS

John MacAulay

There is currently a healthy resurgence of interest in traditional wooden boat-building, but rather in the pursuit of leisure than for serious commercial purposes. The work is confined mainly to individual boat-builders along with an increasing number of enthusiastic amateurs who are keen to learn and retain the craft skills that had so rapidly declined. Indeed there is real concern that those skills could still be lost completely if positive action is not taken. The long-established apprenticeship system which had ensured the continuity of highly-skilled shipwrights and boat-builders is virtually gone, with only a handful of boatyards now remaining which employ craft apprentices on a regular basis. Also at risk is the expertise to sail and even row those boats, and the intimate knowledge of boats and the sea the shipwrights depended on to be able to refine their designs to meet specific needs.

It could be countered that modern boat-building offers training and expertise in a wide range of skills, including naval architecture, but it is doubtful if these could be recognised as true craft skills where the hand and eye of the individual artisan is allowed free expression. Many of today's most successful designs have been modelled on specific boats from a bygone era, and they carry the identity, at least in name, if not truly in character, of the original.

There is a real problem in the lack of an organised training facility in Scotland for people wishing to learn traditional boat-building skills, either as a career or a personal interest.

It would be natural to assume that boat-building always took place where there was an adequate supply of suitable timber. This was true in many instances, and still is in specific regions throughout the world wherever a sustainable supply of material exists. One good example is Norway, in particular the Hardanger Fjord area, regarded as the foundation of Norway's extensive boat-building industry. However, there have been other boat-building areas where absolutely no timber grew. The islands of Shetland, Orkney and the Outer Hebrides, always completely dependent on communication by

Below
Ian Best, boat-builder, Fair Isle.

sea, do not support the means to fabricate any kind of boat apart from the primitive hide-covered curragh or coracle. Yet the finest boats have been built in these islands, at least since the Norse occupation. Some boats were imported from Norway built in 'knock-down' form, dismantled for transportation, and reassembled on arrival. It may be assumed that with these models boat-building skills first developed in the islands.

Sawn timber was later transported from Norway and the Baltic region. If we consider the current situation in Scotland, we find that there are very few places where the right materials exist on the doorstep. We no longer have the specialist sawmills that supplied the boatyards around the coast. Conservation measures also restrict, and rightly so, the availability of timber in certain areas. So regardless of where the craftsman is situated, it is almost inevitable that the raw material has to be hauled from further afield. The other artisans involved – the blacksmith, chandler, rope and sailmaker – who were at the core of every seafaring community have vanished or else relocated to serve the yachting fraternity in modern marina developments. Amazingly, the complex logistics of the boat-building world do not appear to deter the traditional shipwright, and today we can find craftsmen operating in extremely remote locations on the north and west coasts, and in the islands, producing excellent boats which command acclaim at boat shows and maritime festivals, in spite of serious competition from modern builders. Most of them exist for the sheer joy of exercising their craft, rather than to meet market demands, and to develop that special relationship which grows around each boat from the very first day that building commences. This personal identification cannot be equalled by factory production methods and man-made materials.

The majority of boat-builders specialise in a specific type of boat, usually relevant to the area or island group where they live and work. This reflects the traditions of each particular location where boat designs evolved to suit immediate needs: boats for fishing, transport, coastal work and for the open ocean. These are boats which can be recognised anywhere because of specific design characteristics, and which immediately portray the peculiar attributes of a certain craftsman. Conversely, the modern fishing boat-builder is constrained by circumstances to design and build boats to meet stringent safety rules and regulations, rather than to harmonise the natural laws of hydrodynamics, the elements and natural building materials, and the skills of the experienced craftsman.

Probably the easiest to identify by the lay person are the Shetland boats: the *four'ern* and the *six'ern*, their pedigree immediately betrayed, as are also the Stroma and Ness *yole*, from their likeness to the *faering* and *sexaering* of Norway. Any modification to suit local conditions must have been minimal and the fact that they are still popular enough to be replicated in modern materials is testimony to their special qualities.

I had the good fortune to be able to work for some years with the late Tom Edwardson who belonged to the Shetland Isle of Unst. Tom was a craftsman of the old school and would build what he proudly termed 'da Shetland model' entirely by eye, without the use of moulds or templates of any kind. His boats were works of art and highly regarded by his contemporaries. He was also a master at sailing them, and was a frequent competitor at regattas in his time.

On the Hebridean Isle of Lewis a substantially different style of boat evolved in the Ness district. Situated on the exposed northern tip of the island, any boat had to negotiate the wide expanse of the North Minch and the Atlantic. With a fishing area that included the remote outposts of North Rona and Sulasgeir, the boats, the *Sgoth Niseach*, which varied in size from twenty-five feet to around thirty-feet in length, were heavily built in comparison with the Shetland boats. Like all traditional island boats they were clinker-built of larch strakes on grown-oak frames. They were quite full in the beam and relatively high-sided, and were excellent load-carriers, often tested to the limit when returning from the fishing grounds loaded with fish, wet nets, and the normal complement of six or eight crewmen. Ness may well have been the last fishing community where the womenfolk carried the men on their backs through the surf to get them on board dry! Strangely, there was no marked transition from sail to motor in the

history of the *Sgoth Niseach*. Their noble era abruptly ended with a dire shortage of able crewmen following the ravages of the Second World War. Subsequent fishing effort was to be carried out from the main island port of Stornoway on larger drifters and liners.

A thirty-three foot *Sgoth* has recently been built for the Sulaire Trust of Stornoway by John Murdo MacLeod, the last of that Ness family of *Sgoth* builders. Although now retired, John Murdo still keeps his hand in and continues to build the occasional rowing boat.

In May 1999 a one-day exhibition and conference to celebrate the 'Grimsay' boats was organised by Mary Norton on the Isle of Grimsay, North Uist. Three generations of the Stewart family had been boat-builders who devoted their working lives to building one specific type of boat. Many fine examples of their craft can still be seen working the island shores for lobster and crabs, but the old boatyard at Kenary is silent since Angus, the last of that line of craftsmen, died suddenly in June 1994 after finishing his day's work on a new boat. His brother William, also a boat-builder but who chose to spend most of his working life as a fisherman in his self-built boat, is now retired but hopes to see the family tradition revived, and to that end he is actively encouraging a nephew to convert his skills as a joiner to a nobler use.

The Grimsay boat is double-ended and varies in length from twenty-one to around twenty-five feet. Those built originally for the Monach Isles fishing were rigged with two standing lug-sails and a jib. This rig was modified to a single dipping lug-sail when the first internal combustion engines were fitted. The boats adapted quite readily to engine power and could be very easily driven with a paraffin engine of between five and twelve horsepower. They were clinker-built of larch strakes on steam-bent oak ribs and if, in comparison with contemporary craft, they appear at first sight to be less robust, a closer inspection reveals a constructional ingenuity which combines maximum strength with the most economic use of material. Like the majority of Scottish coastal and island boats, they were completely open and depended on the transverse thwarts for lateral rigidity. The Grimsay craftsmen improved on the standard method for securing the ends of the thwarts with grown-oak knees by fitting substantial fore and aft stringers between each thwart end; these were also closely fitted to the hull planking and frames, creating a highly-effective 'ring-frame' giving greatest strength where most needed, but still allowing the hull to flex and absorb the external forces of water pressure acting on the hull. The fine underwater lines allowed the boats to be easily rowed, and their sailing qualities and manoeuvrability were unmatched. With the advent of motor power the design gradually altered and you are now more likely to find a transom-sterned boat with a wider beam and slightly more freeboard in order to accommodate all of the equipment that goes along with today's catching methods.

I recently drafted the lines of the *Welcome Home*, a twenty-three foot Grimsay boat built for the Monach Isles lobster fishing in 1933. Originally built for sail, she was later converted to engine power. Amazingly, there was no more than three-quarters of an inch difference at any point of measurement on either side despite having been built entirely 'by eye' and having been worked hard for around sixty years before being laid up. When newly built by the Stewarts of Kenary and fully fitted out, she cost the handsome sum of thirty-two pounds and ten shillings. The *Welcome Home* is now laid up ashore under cover, awaiting restoration.

The *Sgoth Niseach* and the Grimsay boats are outstanding in the Hebrides in that they are identified with a distinct locality, and both evolved to meet the requirements of their individual environment. In other areas of the islands and the Scottish coast there were designs that reflected certain needs and working conditions, but they have succumbed to modern influences to a greater degree than those in the very remote regions.

The building of traditional clinker-planked boats has changed little since Viking times and, apart from the use of modern machinery to cut and shape the wood, the actual building process remains the same. Many of the builders worked entirely from experience gained over many years, without the use of elaborate moulds to guide them. The building

of a clinker boat, that is where each strake overlaps the previous lower one, commences with the laying of the keel and the raising of the stem and stern posts. These main structural members, usually of oak, have a rebate carved out along each side where the first or garboard strake fits snugly into the keel and where the hood-ends of each strake meet the stem and stern post. The width and shape of each strake varies throughout the boat, as does the amount of winding or twist applied as the hull is shaped. It is necessary to steam the wood in order to soften its fibres, after which it is possible to create complex twisting curves without risk of breakage. After cooling the wood retains this new shape.

The complete hull shell can be planked up before any frames or ribs are fitted. The longitudinal stiffness created by the overlapping strakes, fastened with copper boat-nails, is sufficient to maintain the required shape until the frames are added. In small boats, dinghies and other boats up to around thirty feet in length, where lightness and flexibility is desirable, steam-bent oak ribs are adequate, but for more robust service or for larger boats it is best to build with grown oak frames. The individual frame members are selected from natural crooks or bends that best fit the sections of hull to be framed. They are marked from a template before sawing to shape with the correct bevel, and are stepped or notched to fit the strakes. They can then be nailed through and clenched, or galvanised dumps are driven dead into the frames. The spacing between frames also depends on the degree of strength required and, as can be seen in fishing boats from fifty to eighty feet in length, the grown frames virtually form a solid wall of oak within the hull. In open boats the thwarts or rowing benches are the members which impart transverse rigidity and have to be secured firmly at each end using grown knees, sometimes in pairs, which are riveted to the riser and the gunwale with heavy copper nails. The gunwale itself is secured in like manner at the bow and stern with grown breast-hooks and quarter-knees, closely following the required shape in the natural grain of the wood for maximum strength.

Watertight integrity depends to a great extent on the closeness of finish to each plank overlap or 'land'. The bevels must be extremely accurate and each strake has to be

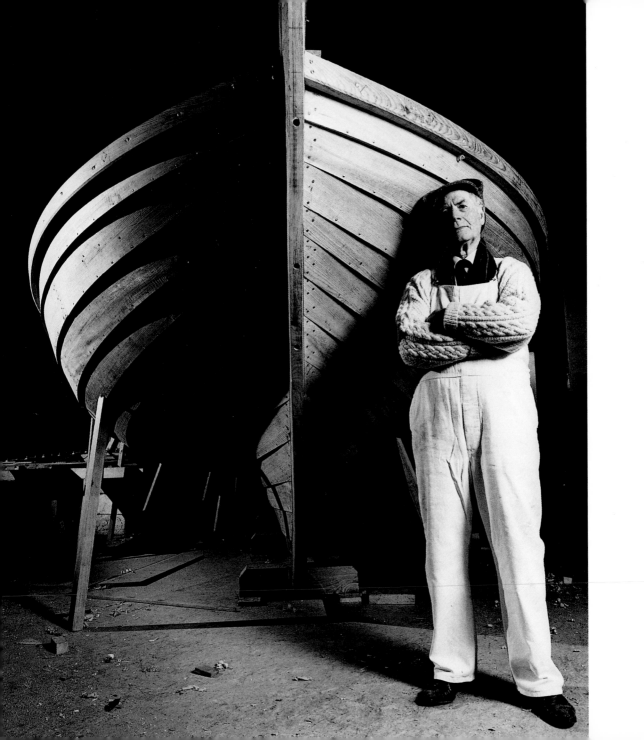

steamed sufficiently to ensure that there is no undue straining before the copper nails are clenched up tight. Normally a seam-dressing of Stockholm tar or an oil varnish between the lands is all that is required to guarantee a watertight fit. However, it is normal practice to caulk the garboard strake and the hood ends with cotton caulking, or oakum in heavier work, and seal it over with a filling compound. In carvel construction, where the frames are set up first and the strakes are added butting flush against each other, it is vital that every seam is well caulked throughout. I recently spoke to an islander who related that his father, a boat-builder, used dried moss with Stockholm tar for caulking his boats – exactly the same as the Norse shipwrights of a thousand years ago!

Present-day materials demand new techniques and, usually, a factory environment. Regardless of the perceived convenience of new products and innovative production methods, there can never be anything to compare with the special relationship that develops with any particular wooden boat. It begins the very first day that building commences and continues to grow throughout the boat's career. There is a bonding that embraces the builder, the owner and all the natural materials that are used which expresses itself in something far deeper than what the eye beholds – almost as if life had been created by the craftsman's hands. And it is that essence which causes people today to succumb to the values of traditional boats and which will ensure continued interest in this ancient craft.

The rapid acceleration in boat production from synthetic material in the last thirty years or so is only now showing its effects on the traditional industry. Many of the long-established boatyards around our coasts have closed down, though some still survive to service the existing fishing fleet. Each passing year sees fewer craftsmen who are skilled in the traditional ways of building wooden boats. The new generation of boat-builders are only familiar with steel or glass-reinforced plastic. The decline is serious and the prospect of revival can only be through an active stimulation of the current interest in these ancient skills.

The transition from sail to steam almost 100 years ago, when iron and steel replaced larch and oak in the larger fishing vessels, was the principal cause of the decline and it is highly unlikely that fishermen could return to those older ways. The future for wooden boat-building can only be with craft enthusiasts who are willing to devote time and energy to the preservation of our maritime cultural heritage in a real and enduring way, by recreating what was once an everyday feature of our coastal life.

Glossary

BEAM	maximum width.
BOAT NAILS	square copper nails.
BREAST-HOOK	grown oak bracket fixing gunwales to stem.
CAULK	to make a watertight seal between each member.
CLINKER	overlapping planks or strakes.
DRIFTER	boat equipped for drift-net fishing.
DUMP	galvanised spike.
FORE AND AFT	extreme ends, or lying in that direction.
FOUR'ERN	four oared boat.
FRAME	individual transverse rib sections.
FREEBOARD	distance from waterline to gunwale.
GARBOARD	lowest strake, next to keel.
GROWN-OAK	grain of wood follows required shape.
GUNWALE	strengthening to uppermost strake.
HOOD-END	end of strake rebated into stem.
KEEL	main structural member, 'backbone'.
KNEE	bracket of grown oak.
LAND	section of strake at each overlap.
LENGTH	overall length, stem to stern.
LINER	boat equipped for long-line fishing.
LINES	the designed shape of a boat.
LUG-SAIL	traditional rig of Scottish fishing boats.
MOULD	cross-section shape of boat.
OAKUM	caulking material of natural fibres.
QUARTER KNEE	grown-oak bracket fixing gunwales to transom.
REBATE	groove in keel to receive garboard strake.
RIB	as frame, but of lighter material.
RISER	fore and aft member to support thwarts.
SIX'ERN	six oared boat.
STEAM BENT	wood softened by heat to facilitate bending.
STEM	forward member, or leading edge.
STERN	rear member.
STOCKHOLM TAR	wood tar, distilled from pine.
STRAKE	individual planks from stem to stern.
STRINGER	fore and aft strengthening inside frames.
TEMPLATE	pattern.
THWART	transverse seat.
TRANSOM	squared-off shape at stern.
YOLE	typical Northern Isles boat.

Further reading

MacAulay, J: *Birlinn, Longships of the Hebrides* (The White Horse Press, 1996).
MacAulay, J: *Seal-Folk and Ocean Paddlers* (The White Horse Press, 1998).

Below

An 'ausker' – a scoop for bailing water from the boat, carved from a single piece of wood.

Opposite

The third strake of a Ness Yole clamped on ready for fastening, in the workshop of Ian Best, Fair Isle.

Through this essay I hope to give some insight into a few of the more interesting aspects of bagpipe-making in Scotland, the related social context, both past and present, and some of the rich and diverse cultural heritage associated with this instrument. Bagpipe-making is both an exacting engineering science and a creative art form requiring a wide range of skills, including a highly developed musical ear. It can be frustrating, but for the most part provides a high degree of satisfaction, a meagre income and a wonderful way of travelling from day to day. I would like to take this opportunity to pay tribute and give thanks to all my family and friends who have been involved in the business, either directly or indirectly over the years – your dedicated work and help has been invaluable.

With the help of my father, David Moore, I started making Scottish small pipes in 1985. Our first sets were sold in 1986 and the business has grown slowly and organically since. To date we have produced 600 sets of pipes and there are currently seven people involved in the production on a self-employed basis. My son Fin joined the firm in June 1997 to serve an apprenticeship.

The business was originally established with the express purpose of manufacturing bellows-blown Scottish small pipes, a culturally important Scottish instrument. Expansion has closely followed and greatly contributed to the ever-growing renaissance of this instrument. During the last five years we have added Highland pipes in the key of A, standard Highland pipes, Border pipes and reel pipes to the varieties made, and in each case we used historically important sets of pipes as models for reconstruction.

Scottish small pipes

Scottish small pipes have led the present revival of bellows-blown pipes nationally and internationally. In its modern form it is a bellows-blown bagpipe with three drones set in a common stock and with a cylindrically-bored open-ended chanter. The drones are

THE MANUFACTURE OF BAGPIPES

Hamish Moore

tuned to the tonic, one an octave below the tonic and one in between, on the fifth. They are currently being made in four keys, namely A, B flat, C and D. The key of A is the most popular and can now be regarded as the standard for this instrument. The scale of the chanter is mixolydian, having a sharpened third and sixth and natural seventh. The pipes are harmonically rich, easy to maintain, and due to a lack of moisture in the system the reeds are very stable and have a life of many years. In the keys of A and B flat, the finger-spacing and pitch are both similar to the practice chanter but with a vastly improved tone. It is little wonder that these pipes have reached their present level of popularity. Once the bellows technique has been mastered, the player has an instrument quiet enough to be played indoors with little physical effort and acoustically and musically compatible with most other instruments.

There is no doubt that small pipes existed in Scotland in various forms (both mouth- and bellows-blown), but these have all suffered a fall into near or complete extinction. The present revival started in 1983 when the celebrated Northumbrian pipe-maker, Colin Ross, designed a Scottish cylindrically-bored open-ended chanter to fit the highly developed and sophisticated Northumbrian chanter reed, but which played with the Highland bagpipe fingering system. The first chanters were made in the key of D for myself and the well-known singer Artie Tresize, who used the pipes to great effect with his singing partner, Cilla Fisher, in their children's show *The Singing Kettle*. Chanters in the other keys of C, A and B flat followed fairly soon and the revival was underway. These developments, given the number of Highland pipers in the world, created a commercially viable situation for the many fledgling pipe-makers who were to start making these pipes professionally. Colin had developed a hybrid instrument which was to form the basis of a renaissance in the Highland piping world as significant as any single event since the inception of the first piping competition in 1781. When we came to start making Scottish small pipes in 1985, we used a set of Highland small pipes as our model for the drones, bellows and bag, rather than the Northumbrian pipes on which Colin had based his instrument. The chanter and reed combination, however, was based on Colin's revolutionary work, although during the intervening

years modifications have been made to the chanter design and the reed has evolved to be quite distinct from the original.

The Border pipes

These pipes are copied from Cox's Plans, *circa* 1740-60. They are bellows-blown, have three drones issuing from a common stock, and have a conical bored chanter in contrast to the parallel bore of the small pipes, thus allowing the pipes to play an octave higher than the quieter and more mellow small pipes. The drone arrangement is A bass, A tenor and high E alto. The key of the chanter is A, and as well as the normal mixolydian scale there are four semitones available, namely B flat, C natural, E flat and F natural. These are achieved only in conical chanters and by the use of a system of cross-fingering. The wood of choice for these pipes is either boxwood, which is grown high in the Pyrenees Mountains, or local yew.

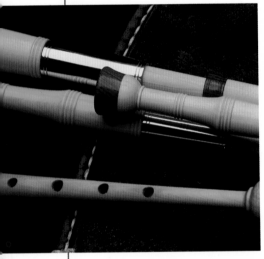

The pipes were traditionally popular on both sides of the border, this being reflected in what was often a common repertoire between the Scottish Borders and Northumberland. In Scotland many of the border towns employed a border piper whose duty it was to play through the streets in the early morning and to sound the curfew at night. The pipes declined in popularity towards the end of the nineteenth century and had virtually died out of use by the beginning of the twentieth century. An interesting phenomenon, which survived until the 1930s or 1940s, was the Boy Scout Pipe Bands in Northumberland playing and marching with Border bagpipes. The pipes for these bands were traditionally supplied by Robertson's, a well-known firm of bagpipe-makers from Edinburgh.

During the course of the present revival, however, it has only been in the last five or six years that these pipes have gained much popularity. The reasons for this are many, not least of which is the recent improvement in the standard of the pipes and in particular the chanter reed which has resulted in an improvement in the sound of the pipes. The majority of people purchasing bellows-blown pipes are Highland pipers and a large part of the attraction for them is to have an instrument which is quiet enough to be played indoors, is in tune, is low maintenance, and is a contrast to their Highland pipes. The small pipes, with their quiet volume and rich tone, provide an ideal alternative. For the first ten years of manufacture, I estimate that ninety-nine per cent of pipes made by us were small pipes. Today the proportion of small pipes to Border pipes is approximately two to one. This is an interesting development and it is worth noting that the increase in orders for Border pipes is largely the result of people who already have small pipes and who are looking for a more challenging and expressive instrument. The pipes are principally being used in multi-instrumental folk bands where they will cut through and blend particularly well with other instruments. In informal traditional music sessions the pipes are also beginning to find a very strong place and there is a potential for their use with classical musicians in an orchestral setting. These uses are far removed from their original function and it is also interesting to note that, as yet, very few people are playing Border music on these pipes. The Lowland and Border Pipers' Society, since its inception, has done an invaluable job in promoting Scottish small pipes and Border pipes.

Reconstruction of eighteenth-century Highland pipes

We have copied a particularly beautiful set of bagpipes, made at the end of the eighteenth century from ebony and mounted in solid silver, and which is now displayed in Inverness Museum. From the fourteenth century until the late seventeenth century, pipes were made from indigenous timbers such as boxwood, yew, laburnum and various fruitwoods. From the end of the seventeenth century until the early years of the twentieth century, as a result of the colonisation of parts of the West Indies, some very fine timbers became available for pipe-making – cocus wood from Jamaica, lignum vitae from various places in the West Indies, and, later, rosewood from Belize, followed by partridge wood from Venezuela. Parallel to, but later than, the developments in the

West Indies, gradually increasing shipments of ebony and rosewood became available
from India and these exotic species progressively displaced the indigenous timbers. The
availability of these woods closely followed the expansion of the British Empire, which in
turn put greater demands on the newly founded and ever-increasing Highland Regiments
with their accelerating demand for more and more bagpipes. Pipe-makers of the day
were extremely busy — business flourished! There is an interesting anecdote from this
period concerning the MacDougals of Aberfeldy. They were approached by the newly
raised regiment of The Black Watch, who ordered twelve sets of pipes for their pipe
band. MacDougals refused to join this new commercial bandwagon and insisted that
all the pipers visit their premises individually to place personal orders for their pipes!

It was in the last two decades of the eighteenth century that a major change in design
came about. The simple but elegant tulip-shaped bells of the drones became square and
angular, the plain turned surfaces were highly decorated with an intricate system of
combing, and external diameters of the drones and stocks became significantly larger.
The late eighteenth century set in The Inverness Museum made of the exotic hardwood,
ebony, must have been one of the last to be made in the old style. When these pipes
were copied and reeded, they were found to play naturally in the key of A. This has
been most useful for people playing with orchestras and has also been put to good use
in folk bands. The full potential of these pipes, however, will only be realised when they

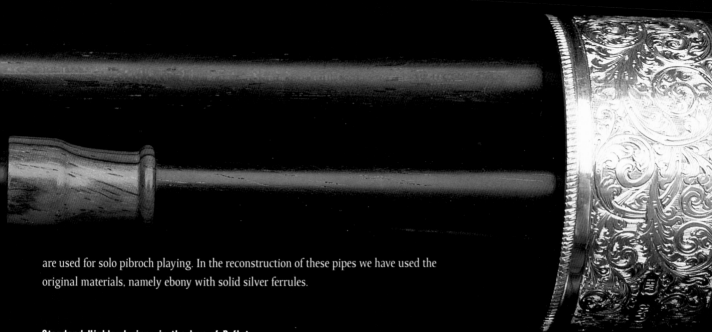

are used for solo pibroch playing. In the reconstruction of these pipes we have used the original materials, namely ebony with solid silver ferrules.

Standard Highland pipes in the key of B flat

The end of the nineteenth to the first third of the twentieth century is generally considered to be the period when the best Highland pipes were made. The standard of the wood was superb and engineering and technical skills were at a level of accuracy that allowed the finest quality of instruments to be made. Therefore it was an early twentieth century set of Peter Henderson drones on which we modelled our standard Highland pipes. This set plays in concert B flat. The original set was made of African blackwood, which became available at the beginning of this century, particularly after the First World War when the United Kingdom took over German East Africa (Tanzania) and the region was opened up to increased commerce. Blackwood came on to the market in increasing quantities and, because of its superior characteristics, has in time displaced ebony. Our reconstructed sets are made from African blackwood, with boxwood providing a beautiful, practical and readily available alternative to ivory for the mounts and ferrules.

Highland reel pipes

The celebrated piper Calum MacPherson from Laggan (1834-1898) played reel pipes and was quoted as expressing his pleasure at being able to play for a dance effortlessly for hours while still being able to smoke his pipe! It appears that these reel pipes were popular in Scotland in the eighteenth and nineteenth centuries. Both Glens of Edinburgh and MacDougals of Aberfeldy advertised them in their catalogues as being either bellows- or mouth-blown. A set of what are probably MacDougals, at present housed in the Piping Centre Museum in Glasgow, gave us the extremely fine example to base our sets on. Because of the great advantages of bellows-blown pipes over mouth-blown, we restrict our manufacture to bellows-blown only. The museum pipes have two tenor drones and one bass drone issuing from a common stock with a conical bore chanter, and are made from what appears to be a fruitwood with horn mounts and ferrules. Our contemporary copies are made from yew with boxwood mounts. Reel pipes were made as a Highland instrument for Highland pipers who would have played a Highland repertoire.

Materials and methods – some brief musings

The wood used in the manufacture of bagpipes is of vital importance to the quality of the instrument. A rigorous selection process followed by an appropriate period of seasoning is essential prior to manufacture of the pipes. Only the finest quality wood should be used: the instrument will last forever and the cost of the wood is only a small percentage of the total cost. The stability of the instrument is dependent largely on two factors: the moisture content of the wood and the inherent forces present in the wood as a result of stresses present in the tree when it was alive. The changes, which happen to the wood as it seasons, must be allowed to take place prior to the final manufacturing process. If the wood is incorrectly or insufficiently seasoned the consequences will be profound, with the possibility of cracks developing, vital internal dimensions changing (most especially in the chanter where even quite small changes can have a large effect), ferrules coming loose under shrinking supporting surfaces, round bores becoming oval in shape and causing mechanical problems, as in the tuning slides of the drones.

Seasoning should take place ideally in a temperature- and humidity-controlled environment over a period of years. The wood should be rough-turned and stored in such a manner that a maximum amount of air circulates around the wood. Where appropriate, a pilot hole should be bored in the wood to allow maximum evaporation of moisture from the wood. Boxwood presents its own special difficulties and is extremely prone to bending. It is, however, a valuable resource with a beautiful appearance and acoustic properties which are second to none. A system of microwaving the wood has been devised to minimise the bending. The wood is brought to boiling-point as quickly as possible and kept close to 100 degrees centigrade for forty-five minutes. Wood that is destined to be made into a mouth-blown instrument is then submerged in a bath of water for one hour before being left to dry for a month. Wood that will be made into dry-blown pipes is at this stage submerged in linseed oil. The theory behind microwaving is simply that the sap is boiled off, rupturing the cellular structure of the wood and relieving the stress present within it, therefore allowing it to bend. The water or oil is absorbed and occupies the inter-cellular spaces. The oil helps to add stability to the wood and water evaporates to an equalised level with the environmental humidity. After bending has taken place the wood is trued-up by re-turning between centres. In the majority of cases the wood is at this point stable and no further bending takes place.

Although meticulous care is taken in the seasoning of the wood, dimensional changes will take place under extremes of temperature and humidity. The moisture content of the wood will only ever be proportional to the relative humidity of the environment. So, for example, if pipes were seasoned and made in Scotland and sent to the Eastern seaboard of the United States in the winter where the relative humidity is extremely low, problems will be encountered unless precautionary humidifying measures are implemented.

The quality of sound of any reeded woodwind instrument, given the fact that the internal dimensions are accurate and the wood is of a certain quality, is largely dependent on the reeds. Cane (*sp Arundo Donax*) is the material of choice and although this species is common throughout Europe there are specific areas where the quality is superior. The best cane for the purposes of my reed manufacture comes from the south of France. There are many factors involved in the cane quality, namely the mineral content of the soil, the weather conditions during any particular growing season (the cane requires a certain period of sustained minimum temperature as well as an exposure to frost), the method of storing and seasoning the cane, and the time of harvesting. This last factor is an interesting one. In Sardinia, where cane is used in the making of the Launedas (a triple pipe with two chanters and one drone), the wild cane fields are jealously guarded by the makers and the cane is only harvested in the months of January or February and only at a full moon! This is not as strange as it may at first seem; the lunar cycle having an effect on all water, it must of course have an effect on the sap in the cane. There are great demands for good quality cane not only from reed-makers for the oboe, bassoon, saxophone and clarinet, but from manufacturers of cane furniture and cane fishing rods. Obtaining good cane is exceedingly difficult; being able to recognise good cane in its raw state and prior to time spent on manufacture is even more difficult and requires almost a sixth sense. Bagpipe-making, like life, is difficult.

Glossary

CHANTER	the pipe on a bagpipe on which the melody is played.
DRONES	the pipes on a bagpipe which sound a constant accompanying note.
MIXOLYDIAN	a musical mode where the third and sixth notes of the scale are sharp and the seventh note is a semitone flat.
PILOT HOLE	a hole bored in wood, of a smaller diameter than the final diameter, which allows the evaporation of moisture from its surfaces, thus accelerating the seasoning process.

Background photograph
Detail of Border pipe drones and chanter.

Inset photograph
Hamish Moore testing a set of
small pipes.

Addresses

THE LOWLAND AND BORDER PIPERS' SOCIETY —
established almost twenty years ago by a small group of enthusiasts, with the aim of promoting
and fostering interest in the pipes of the Borders and their related repertoire.

Contact:
Jim Buchanan, The Secretary,
The Lowland and Borders Pipers' Society
2A Manse Road, Roslin,
Midlothian EH25 9LF

THE PIPING CENTRE —
a centre of excellence of piping in Scotland.

Contact:
30-34 McPhater Street, Glasgow G4 0HW

Hamish Moore, Fungarth Steading, Dunkeld, Perthshire PH8 0ES
Telephone: 01350 727474

Acknowledgements

The author wishes to acknowledge, in particular, Hugh Cheape,
Colin Ross and David Moore for their generous assistance and
sharing of information over the years.

Important early evidence of basketry in Scotland still has to be drawn together into a consistent and analytical account, and the reconstruction in 1998 of a wickerwork shrine for the 'Ballachulish goddess' in the Museum of Scotland recalls that when the wooden figure itself (dated to 730-520 BC) was exhumed from the peat in 1880, it was found to be enclosed in a basketwork 'coffin'. It may be significant and it is certainly intriguing that burials in wicker coffins have been found in many places in the Highlands and Islands, for example in the crypt of Iona Cathedral, and have taken place in Morvern (within sight of the Ballachulish find-spot), almost within living memory. Here also the term *caisil-chrò* has been recorded for a type of basketwork coffin.

By leading with the phrase 'Creels and Sculls', we locate ourselves firmly within the Scottish tradition with an investigation of form and function in basket-making in Scotland. Such multi-functional containers and carrying and transport devices are evident in many forms from prehistoric societies into the present day, and baskets in their varieties of forms are typical products of material culture and of human history. The 'creel' is a deep wicker basket carried on the backs of people or of animals and was used in a roadless countryside for transporting peats, potatoes, fish, or personal goods and chattels. The 'scull' is a shallow basket of wickerwork used for agricultural purposes such as gathering potatoes or stones off the fields, and in a specific form in Scotland as a shallow basket for fishing lines.

Against this historical significance we have the frailty of the evidence. The organic nature of basketry means that it does not readily survive except in extremes of circumstance of very dry or waterlogged and acidic conditions. The National Museums of Scotland have a rich and important collection of baskets, largely the creation of an ornithologist, the late Dr Evelyn Baxter (1879-1959), but augmented significantly since the acquisition of this collection in 1961. As a keen observer of her surroundings, she was struck by variations in form and basket-making techniques in different parts of the country and built up a remarkable collection on her travels in tracking patterns of bird migration.

CREELS AND SKULLS
FORM AND FUNCTION

Vanessa Morris
and Hugh Cheape

The National Museums' catalogues demonstrate a national coverage of Scotland and significant variations both in form and function. Baskets from East Lothian and the Forth Estuary, for example, reflect the historical importance respectively of both gardening and market gardening in this better-endowed area of the country; we find, for instance, a miniature wickerwork basket and a gardener's 'arm-creel' type of basket from East Lothian. Fishing is represented with, notably, Greatlin' Baskets and line sculls or 'murlins' from Newhaven; local information with a number of items from the fishing community of Musselburgh in East Lothian described them as being made from 'wands cropped on Pinkie Braes'. The East Coast from Dundee to Aberdeen is well represented also by fishing baskets such as line sculls from Arbroath, Johnshaven and Inverbervie, and by more modest and less clearly identifiable items such as a peg basket from Dundee itself.

The North West Highlands and Islands including Skye and the Hebrides are represented by regionally specific material such as peat creels. The creel made from hazel or whole or split rods of willow could always be built into a large container. Techniques of building it were simple but sure-handed. For lightness and to ease lifting, one or more rows of 'windows' were left unwoven in the sides of the creel (known in Gaelic as *breagan*). Creels for carrying seaweed as manure for the fields were made more open in construction and even given a hinged base for quick unloading and hopefully lessening back strain. Hugh Miller, mason and geologist, writer and journalist, in describing a village in the North West Highlands about 1823 in an article in *The Witness*, mentions this latter type of creel as a familiar item of local material culture and places it in the often harsh social and economic context of self-reliance: 'The ground was turned up by the spade … and the manure was carried out in spring and the produce brought home in autumn, mostly by women in slip-bottomed creels.' Their form and function in such extreme conditions means that few or none of such items have survived.

But here also we have unusual and distinctive items such as a hen basket from Wester Ross and two smaller baskets from Skye, one of which is described in the catalogues as

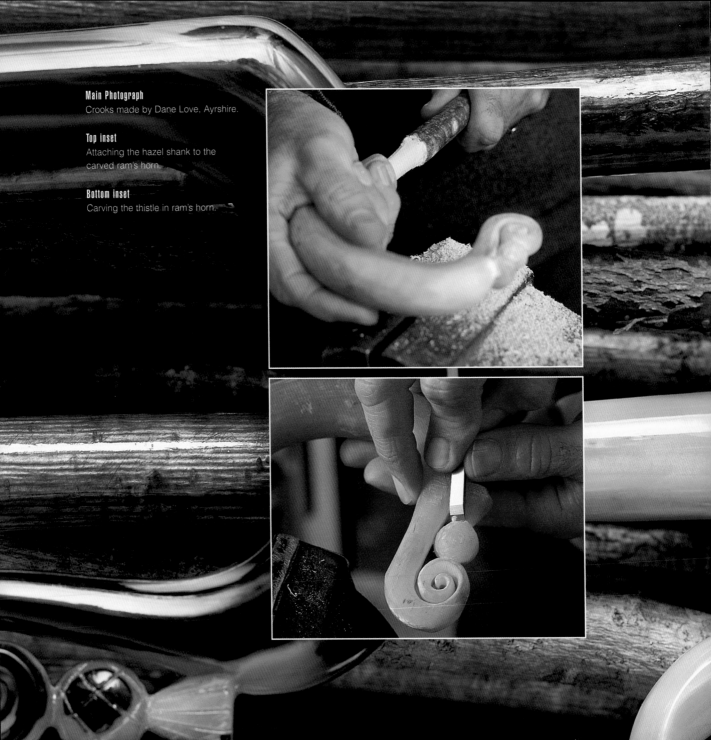

Main Photograph
Crooks made by Dane Love, Ayrshire.

Top inset
Attaching the hazel shank to the carved ram's horn.

Bottom inset
Carving the thistle in ram's horn.

a wickerwork wool basket or 'crealagh' in the shape of a rugby ball. This information may not be reliable and should be questioned; a preferred name for this type of basket is 'mudag' which carries the authority of dictionary definition and is more widely recognised together with dialect variation such as 'murlag', a term traditionally used in Argyll. The Northern Isles of Orkney and Shetland are well represented and the collections have been significantly augmented in recent years by contributions to the Saxby-Sandison Collection from Unst; this includes baskets commissioned from traditional makers, and in every instance a careful record of provenance has been made by the donor together with relevant lexical and linguistic information. The Northern Isles material gives the immediate impression of a rich variety of objects made from different raw materials and designed for specific uses. Examples are the docken or 'bulmint' buddie from Shetland, used for carrying fish, a muck kishie from Shetland for carrying dung to the fields, seaweed from the shore, messages from the shop and other crofting work, or an oval straw basket, bound with 'simmens' of bent grass, from Papa Westray, Orkney.

The kishie is worn on the back, with the band across the chest, leaving the hands free for work. Lawrence Copland, now in his seventy-sixth year in Shetland, has been making kishies all his life. It was part of the natural rhythm of crofting life to make straw kishies during the winter months and Lawrence learnt the craft from his father, as he in turn had learnt from his father before him. Although built for rigorous daily use, the kishie makers took great pride in their craft. Lawrence recounted how 'crops were often calculated by kishie-fills. I remember the summer of 1947 was exceptionally good, and we had a tally of 416 kishies of tatties that year'. He continues to make and teach the local community the skills of making the kishie.

In the social and economic continuum of medieval Scotland, nearly every material need of farm and township was satisfied by the work of the family and the local community, and this self-sufficiency only began to break down in the course of the agricultural and industrial revolutions. Clothing, food of course, implements, tools and utensils such as

Below
Lawrence Copland of Shetland
with his 'docken kishie'.

Opposite
Jimmy Work of Shetland.

typically baskets and containers, furniture, buildings and dwelling-houses were fashioned locally and with local materials. Where there was a specialist (as we would understand the word), it was usually the maker of edged tools: the blacksmith, a figure held in high esteem and occupying a special position in the community. There were others who did specialist work within recorded history, such as the tinkers, or 'travelling folk', since they could not be supported by the work available in any one district. Tinsmithing, horncraft and baskets have traditionally been their stock in trade and there are memories of travelling basket-makers, mainly in the East of Scotland, making and repairing potato sculls, for example.

The contemporary practice of this indigenous craft still sustains a strong social element: the decision to make not only out of necessity for supporting the family but also to perpetuate a way of life which is in harmony with local history, wishing not to maintain a myth but a living culture much as we attempt to do every day in museums. The National Museums of Scotland collects and documents Scottish basketry in all its forms, including the contemporary basket that bridges areas between the functional and pure aesthetic forms.

The museums also have the self-assumed responsibility of collecting not just the things but the names of things. Instigated by German philologists and ethnologists in the late-nineteenth century, the study of words and their meanings was introduced into cultural history. Through an interdisciplinary approach and the study of language, the distribution of objects and their variant forms could then be mapped with relevant words and names to throw light on cultural patterns and historical change. Language is embraced by the contemporary basket-maker who continues to use these names and terms when making like forms. However, terms recovered in the search for origins may be deceptive, and what appears to be primary evidence of words and terminology has often been misinterpreted; also the contemporary maker may use apparently localised names even if this is not exactly the geographical location in which the original type of basket of this name was made and where the design might have developed over time.

There is a strong likelihood in Scotland that the name of an object collected for the museums would not be in Standard English. It would either be in a dialect of Northern English, of varieties of Scots, or of Orkney or Shetland, or that it would be in another language, quintessentially of course in Gaelic or one of its dialects. In practice we find a wide range of terms being used and a basket is evidently not just a 'basket'. For example, in one island alone, containers of bent grass or muran have been referred to by names such as 'rusgan', 'mudag', 'mugan', 'ciosan', 'caiteag' or 'seic'. Generally the lexicographers of Gaelic were not attuned to the practical level of material culture, yet the terminology of material culture is remarkably rich. In checking the word 'crealagh' (mentioned above) applied to the wool basket from Skye in the collections of the National Museums of Scotland, it does not appear to be in any of the standard Gaelic dictionaries, although the form *craidhleag* can be found and the different spelling must be significant. We should ask ourselves what the significance therefore is of this name, whether it is an otherwise unrecorded dialect variant, or whether it is a 'ghost-word' surfacing in less than rigorous recording and scholarship. Taking terms such as 'creel' and 'scull', we find that they are both specific names as well as generics, depending not only on the type of basket but also the context and dialect area in which it is being used. But this is not necessarily the case when, for example the 'tattie-scull' typical of East coast usage became a 'creel o coal' to stoke the bothy fire.

This 'home industry' of basket-making, either of local or travelling folk, depended on wood and other plant products in the natural resources that lay to hand. Rushes, grasses, heather, firwood, birch, hazel and willow were the commonly-used natural materials for this work. In most parts of Scotland, for example, marram grass (or muran) had many uses and was used in basketry. A coiling technique made seed baskets, bee skeps, pony mats, and even the seats and backs of chairs in a richly developed art using ties of split briar which was a very labour-intensive skill. Innately part of the self-reliance of traditional communities was a vast store of knowledge about trees, plants, animals, birds and fishes; interest in this world of nature taught that everything had a practical or medicinal, even magical use. Basket-makers today often work in isolation, drawing inspiration from this diverse tradition and from its landscape, the source of their raw materials, but also cradling the social context in which their baskets are made.

Opposite
Stages in the making of 'simmens'.

The virtues sought of a basket are that it should be strong but light, multi-functional within reason, generally but not exclusively 'tight', in other words that it might be capable of holding substance such as meal ground fine between quern or millstones. Form therefore generally follows function, although the availability of raw materials will significantly affect this. For the contemporary basket-maker who makes a living from this craft, much time is spent growing, harvesting and treating to achieve a raw material which will work sympathetically with the hand and not fight against it. The selection of material was not so considered in earlier instances. However, in all cases the basket-maker responds to the material at hand, and with the availability of more refined materials the design and finish of these baskets is evolving. Willow is now the dominant material used in the craft of basketry. There are hundreds of varieties of willows (*Salix*) and it is used for its distinctive characteristics which in turn determine the structure and making process of a basket.

Due to the wealth of material to hand, the indigenous Scottish basket-making tradition has remained alive. The raw materials used now in their many forms – willow, hazel, larch, pine needles, honeysuckle – offer a variety of organic material that has the potential to be twined, woven or plaited to form a 'basket', either as an aesthetic object or a functional basket. All of the practitioners use traditional techniques and historical baskets form the starting point, adapting and re-interpreting them to exploit the immense aesthetic potential of the medium. Much more colour has been introduced into basket-making by the willow treatments, hedgerow materials and the use of natural and artificial dyes; colour was hardly a concern of the functional basket in history. There is however still no mechanical process to imitate the work of the basket-maker, only the hand can dictate when to lessen the tension in the weaves or alter the design, the pattern and strength in a particular piece by a change in technique as the basket 'grows'.

In the past, form reflected function; baskets were made from materials gathered locally for use in the home and workplace. The styles of baskets evolved more out of the need for efficiency and productivity rather than as an act of individual expression and creativity. In the past such a craft existed and developed through its role in the working and domestic lives of the people, drawing on a sense of community and shared passion for tradition and material to move forward. The sharing of knowledge and skills in basket-making has not and does not yet exist within academic circles or institutions in Scotland.

Changes in Scotland over the last two hundred years – the destruction of woodland, the spread of mono-culture (such as the potato, bringing famine in its wake), emigration and the abandonment of community values, the arrival of mass-produced goods, the spread of formal education and book learning – have resulted in the evaporation of traditional and ancient knowledge. But the contemporary basket-maker is perpetuating the traditions of his craft in spite of such sweeping changes and the sense of loss and cultural impoverishment. The Scottish Basketmakers Circle, formed in 1988, is an organisation dedicated to promoting basket-making and allied crafts in Scotland and includes members who are full-time makers as well as others who are interested in basket-making as a creative hobby. This organisation tries to fulfil the role of the old local community in encouraging self-reliance and the sharing of knowledge. Today the style of a basket, whether functional or non-functional, evolves from a response to materials and to a client's individual needs and expectations, as well as with the self-expression of the maker. The contemporary basket-maker is continuing this tradition, raising the status of this remarkable traditional craft while integrating new materials and forms.

Rural crafts have their roots deep in a past of Scottish history and prehistory. Their survival we presume over millennia and into an era of new production and design methods must be a testament to high levels of local skill and the use of appropriate and readily available materials. We may also presume that the individuality of craft-work, its labour-intensive character, and the time needed to prepare the raw materials, are factors which, perhaps paradoxically, have ultimately nurtured these crafts and protected them from mass-production. Skills, materials and design have not, however, remained fixed in some bygone age. To analyse and understand Scotland's crafts we must recognise a number of elements such as geography, available resources and materials, and regional economies and the dynamics of the community, all of which influence hand-crafted works made by an individual. Here, in a historical context, we can glimpse current practices and lines of development in the indigenous crafts of Scotland.

Though the land is the product of geophysical forces and nature, it has also been uniquely shaped by its occupancy and geography. A glance at any map of Scotland will leave an instant impression of the prominence of sea and mountains, creating natural highways and fishing grounds in the first and barriers to communication and natural grazing country in the second. These conditioned where people lived and what they did, and folk husbanded materials and honed craft-skills in a largely rural and subsistence economy.

The population of Scotland has been estimated at just over one million at the time of the Union of 1707 and, though fluctuating in the vicissitudes of famine and strife in the course of the seventeenth century, it was generally able to feed itself; the people of Scotland, in the words of Sir Thomas Craig writing in 1605, enjoyed a 'Rough Plenty'. This was upset from time to time when dearth struck and Craig described the circumstance as normal when: 'Should there be a bad harvest, the Highlanders are able to supply us with cheese, which is often used, and without any injury to health, when the supply of cereals is short.' This self-sufficiency and interdependence could be fatally shattered, as in the long unremitting 'Ill Years' or 'King William's Years' of the 1690s

CRAFTS AND CROFTS IN CONTEXT

Hugh Cheape

when perhaps a fifth of the people were forced out of their homes and the population of many parishes fell by a half. The memory of these years long persisted and encouraged measures of agricultural improvement in the opening decades of the eighteenth century, but for most people, work tasks and skills and the round of the seasons still varied little.

The man-made context of this experience and toil differed surprisingly little across the whole land, Lowland and Highland, in which the population was then much more evenly spread with more than fifty per cent living north of the Tay and probably about thirty per cent of the total belonging to the Gaelic-speaking Highlands and Islands; this now unfamiliar demographic structure was to change dramatically when the 'industrial revolution' drew the bulk of the people into the central belt of Glasgow and Edinburgh. The pattern of settlement of this earlier self-sufficient population is represented by variations on a theme of the township, the 'fermtoun' or *baile*, clustered or scattered depending on the lie of the land, and surrounded by the intensively cultivated 'infield' and the variously cropped and exploited 'outfield'.

Though not a homogeneous group, the tenants of the township formed the backbone of rural society, each tenant occupying a share of the land, say one or two oxgates (that is, land sufficient for one ox) and contributing the oxen as draught animals to the common plough. Below the fermtoun tenants in a rural hierarchy were sub-tenants and cottars, though generally all had some direct share in the land. The main infield and outfield crops were oats and bere (an older form of barley), and the livestock were cattle, sheep and goats. The occupations and common interests of this group bound their lives together to give them a historical and geographical coherence of the greatest significance for the social and economic history of Scotland and for the transmission of their cultural traditions. Much of the major seasonal work such as ploughing and winning of peat for fuel was carried out co-operatively, and most craft-work was done by the community itself either in response to domestic and local needs or as part of the payment of rents in kind and in services. Craft production traded commonly in the busy world of the fairs and markets, popular landmarks in time and space throughout the whole country and traditionally held on the festivals and saints' days of the medieval church and still widely commemorated after the Reformation.

Typical of local crafts, both for home consumption and for the market, were the preparation of wool for weaving and the spinning and weaving of flax into linen. Much of this was done within the home to supply family needs, the bride's providing or 'tocher', and also 'ells of cloth' to be paid as rent and traditionally supplementing the laird and his lady's napery. The only constraints on this busy domestic industry were township regulations, for example against the 'retting' or steeping of flax in running water. So widespread were these textile-working skills that they were already a staple product of the Scottish economy in the late medieval period and formed the foundation of the first phases of the 'industrial revolution' until the widespread adoption of mill and machine spinning and weaving in the first half of the nineteenth century. The rural

and domestic craft of weaving grew into a trade in the eighteenth century and flourished until the 1830s. The parish Statistical Accounts of the 1790s show how every burgh and country community was by then full of 'websters' or weavers: for example, the country parish of Alvie in Strathspey numbered six weavers, four tailors, two brogue-makers and two smiths.

Blacksmiths had always been a vital part of this craft community, making and repairing tools and implements and shoeing horses. Most tools were made of wood, and even the big eight or twelve oxen ploughs were all wooden except for their coulters, socks and bridles and soam (draught) chains. The blacksmith supplied what was described as the 'pleuch graith' (plough irons) and commonly the raw material was supplied by the customers themselves and payment in kind often sought in the form of worked iron for re-use. Many old blacksmiths' swage blocks have a range of moulds in them, for example typically a cruisie lamp mould, showing that they would also fashion goods for domestic use including items such as 'snecks' for door furniture. Other common rural crafts were wood-working and coopering, leather-working and basketry. In the course of the 'agricultural revolution', rural craft-work was augmented significantly by new species of tradesmen such as millwrights and masons, and the craft domain of the blacksmith expanded with the development of new iron agricultural implements such as the all-iron 'swing plough' which became common from the 1780s. A good impression of the self-sufficiency as well as the interdependency of the community with regard to craft-work before the 'agricultural revolution' is conveyed by a list of farm implements used on a typical family farm in Caithness and Sutherland in the eighteenth century: they had a plough, two pairs of harrows, a digging spade, two 'flauchter' or turf spades, four wooden shovels, two 'ceabas' or mattocks, an iron soam for the ox plough, four 'cellach' carts, four straw horse collars, four hair halters, four crook saddles (for creels and baskets), four sets of horsehair traces, two flails, wechts (sieves), riddles and shearing hooks. It is clear that the farmer contributed to the large township ox plough, but he also may have used the 'cas chrom' or foot-plough and had four small horse for fetching and carrying and to assemble the four-horse plough team more typical of Highland farming. It can be assumed that most of this equipment was made by the family for communal use with some input from a blacksmith.

As rural crafts-folk became a more distinct group, especially in the course of the eighteenth century – whether as smith, wright, weaver, tailor or soutar – they were also still farmers and crofters with a stake in the land. It is evident that as far back as the records can tell us most craft-workers held a piece of land in return for the services of their respective crafts; often these were allocated at very low rental as crofts and 'pendicles' (smallholdings) on poorer land on the margins of settlements and the occupiers were expected to break in the ground for cultivation. An exception to these circumstances for every community were nomadic craft-workers, the 'tinker' folk whose traditional crafts were in metal and horn. As well as supplying seasonal labour in the townships, their traditional skills were in making household items, pots, cans, lids and lanterns of tinware, hornware such as spoons, and also baskets. 'If ye mairry a tink,' as the proverb said, 'ye maun cairry the cans.'

Shelter was a fundamental imperative on the Atlantic seaboard and northern edge of Europe and every family was accustomed and inherently skilled to building and furnishing their own dwelling. The main components were the cruck-frames or 'couples' in most parts of the country, and these were generally the most valuable item among the tenants' goods and gear and flitted with him. As large pieces of timber they became increasingly valuable as the country's forest cover shrank. In many areas and especially on the big estates and clan territories, woods were generally reserved for the laird and feudal superior and their use was in turn controlled by his feudal court and policed by his 'ground officer'.

Land granted by the king to his subjects carried rights of jurisdiction which were exercised in a 'baron's court' which historically played an important role in the rural economy. The tenants of the barony were bound when summoned to attend the baron's court, which was presided over by the laird as baron or his baillie having power to settle

disputes and exact fines, and regulating *inter alia* the use of pasture and grazings, muirs and mosses, and trees and forest. The enforcement of regulations is a measure of their concern with the economic life of the community and the keeping of what was described as 'guid nichtbourheid', that is the tenants' requirement to husband the community's resources and to perform their share of the labour of the township. Trees were a vital community and craft resource to hand and barons' courts are frequently seen protecting them and imposing fines for cutting, for example, 'green wood'; in 1722 the Court of Balgair in Stirlingshire in the rural centre of Scotland typically 'ordains the haill tennents to take caire of the haill trees within their possessione that non of them be distroyed under the penaltie of fyftie pounds Scotts attoure paying the damnadges done'. The role of the barons' courts in the agricultural system and the rural economy was a vital one, and until their virtual abolition under the terms of the Heritable Jurisdictions Act of 1747 much can be learnt about crafts and craft-work in the community in their surviving records.

In so many of its facets a largely subsistence rural economy persisted, but it was not altogether a static or unchanging one and areas such as the Lothians adjacent to larger burghs and the cities experienced considerable social and economic change. Recent research (cited below) has proposed a more dynamic model of Scottish agricultural society. Generally, however, most burghs were small places and the line between town and country was less distinct; many townsfolk were farmers with shares in arable rigs and stock pastured on the burgh muir and all townsfolk were dependent on the countryside for grain, flesh, fish and its craft production such as woodwork and basketry. Depending on supplies of materials, most craft-work remained unchanged throughout the subsequent periods of agricultural and industrial revolutions until new ideologies emerged, independently of conditions of demand and supply, to shift practice and perception in the late nineteenth and early twentieth centuries.

Further reading

Alexander, William: *Notes and Sketches Illustrative of Northern Rural Life in the Eighteenth Century* (Edinburgh, 1877).

Barron, Douglas Gordon (ed): *The Court Book of the Barony of Urie in Kincardineshire, 1604-1747* (Scottish History Society, Edinburgh, 1892).

Dunlop, Jean: *Court Minutes of Balgair* (Scottish Record Society, Edinburgh, 1957).

Fenton, Alexander: *Scottish Country Life* (Edinburgh, 1976).

Grant, I F: *Everyday Life on an Old Highland Farm* (London, 1924, 1981).

Grant, I F and Hugh Cheape: *Periods in Highland History* (London, 1987, 1997).

Gunn, Clement B (ed): *Records of the Baron Court of Stitchill, 1655-1807* (Scottish History Society, Edinburgh, 1905).

Hamilton, Henry (ed): *Selections from the Monymusk Papers (1713-1755)* (Scottish History Society, Edinburgh, 1945).

Sanderson, Margaret H B: *Scottish Rural Society in the Sixteenth Century* (Edinburgh, 1982).

Sinclair, Sir John: *General View of the Agriculture of the Northern Counties* (Edinburgh, 1795).

Symon, J A: *Scottish Farming Past and Present* (Edinburgh, 1959).

Thomson, J Maitland (ed): 'The Forbes Baron Court Book, 1659-1678' in *Miscellany of the Scottish History Society*, vol III (Scottish History Society, Edinburgh, 1919), pp 203-321.

Whyte, Ian: *Agriculture and Society in Seventeenth Century Scotland* (Edinburgh, 1979).

Louise Butler

Now based in the Scottish Borders, Louise Butler has worked as an independent curator since 1987. She previously held curatorial posts at museums in Tyne and Wear and The Embroiderers Guild at Hampton Court Palace, with a period as Andrew Mellon Research Fellow at The Metropolitan Museum of Art (Costume Institute). Originally working as a women's wear designer, her main interests are costume, textiles and contemporary crafts – with a particular respect for Scotland's indigenous crafts.

Anne Campbell

Born and educated in the Isle of Lewis, Anne Campbell trained at Edinburgh College of Art, graduating in 1984 with a first class honours degree and post-graduate diploma with distinction in drawing and painting. In 1989 she moved to the Isle of Harris to learn traditional skills and worked as a weaver of hand-spun woollen cloth. She moved back to Lewis in 1998, bought a croft and is currently painting full time.

Hugh Cheape

Coming from Angus and West Inverness-shire, Hugh Cheape joined the National Museum of Antiquities of Scotland in 1974 and worked on the setting up of the Scottish Agricultural Museum. During this time he worked with the craft collections of the former Country Life section of the museum. From 1991 he was involved in the Museum of Scotland project. He has published extensively worldwide through essays and research papers, many of which focus on the collections of the National Museums of Scotland.

Stephen Jackson

Stephen Jackson read history at Cambridge before studying Scottish furniture at St Andrews University. He began his museum career at the Grange Museum of Community History in London, later joining the Ceramics and Glass Department at the Victoria and Albert Museum. He became Curator of Scottish and European Furniture at the National Museums of Scotland in 1999.

John MacAulay

John MacAulay is a shipwright who now lives and works on his native Isle of Harris, building wooden boats in the traditional manner and using mainly hand tools. He is also a historian and the author of three books on island culture and heritage, highlighting the links between the Outer Hebrides and Norway since Viking times.

Peter MacDonald

Peter MacDonald is a published tartan historian and weaver, with special expertise in the development and techniques of tartan-weaving and its associated history. Living in Perthshire, he is probably the last hand-weaver in Scotland weaving tartan using a broad range of traditional techniques. His award-winning work has been exhibited and demonstrated worldwide. Design commissions include work for British Airways and the Scottish Tourist Board. He was textile and costume consultant for the film 'Rob Roy'.

Doreen MacIntyre

Doreen MacIntyre is a freelance marketing and environmental consultant. A keen personal interest in traditional and contemporary uses of plants and other natural materials in Scotland recently led to research for an MSc dissertation. The impetus for this research came from her involvement with Edinburgh's Royal Botanic Garden, *Flora Celtica* initiative, which aims to research and publicise the uses of native flora in Celtic countries.

Hamish Moore

Hamish Moore has been playing music and making bagpipes professionally since 1986. Through his recordings, teaching and pipe-making, he has done much to promote the bellows-blown pipes of Scotland. Due to the social, political and religious history of Scotland, much of the rich, colourful diversity of piping culture has been tragically lost. Hamish has been at the forefront of a renaissance promoting a pre-military style of piping, achieved principally through his integrated approach to teaching music through the medium of Gaelic song and as part of the old step dance rhythms. Founder of many piping schools in Scotland and the USA, inspiration and musical director of the Ceolas summer school in South Uist and principal tutor of Scottish Small Pipes at the Gaelic College, Cape Breton 1992-96, Hamish has also published many recordings of his work.

Vanessa Morris

Vanessa Morris is Curator of Contemporary Crafts for the National Museums of Scotland, Edinburgh. Originally tutored in Three Dimensional Design in Glass with Ceramics at Sunderland University, she moved into Arts administration working as a Craft Development Officer for Nottingham County Council and later for Dumfries and Galloway Council. She has also been employed on a freelance basis for consultation for crafts development within Scotland. Her main interests are in finding new ways to present exhibitions, commissions and events, developing the ways a maker can engage with various communities, in different situations and contexts.

Margaret Stuart

Margaret Stuart has, through close family ties, a life-long interest in the history and crafts of the Shetland Isles. Her successful knitwear company, Shetland from Shetland, has had considerable influence on the islands' knitwear industry. She owns a unique collection of historic knitting and artefacts and seizes every opportunity to promote Shetland crafts at home and abroad. The Museum of Shetland Life and the Museum of Shetland Textiles were opened in her extended house to summer visitors. Margaret is a member of the Scottish Arts Council Crafts Committee, has been a judge of handcrafts at the Royal Highland Show on several occasions and has lectured and contributed to books on her subject.

Rosemary Wilkes

Rosemary Wilkes graduated from Edinburgh University in 1968, MA (Hons) Fine Art. She took up spinning, dyeing and Fair Isle knitting in the 1970s and has taught these subjects since the early 1980s. She is past President of the Edinburgh Guild of Weavers, Spinners and Dyers and has held the post of Handcrafts Supervisor at The Royal Highland Show since 1988. Living in East Lothian, she is a keen organic gardener and grows many dye plants.

ACKNOWLEDGEMENTS

Grateful thanks are due to a large number of people who have given generously of their time, advice and enthusiasm to 'Scotland's Crafts'. The Editor wishes particularly to thank all contributors to the book, Shannon Tofts for his wonderful images, Helen Bennett, Mark Blackadder, Jacquie Clapperton, Dale Idiens, Helen Kemp, Colin McCallum, Vanessa Morris, Morag Robertson, Mary Norton Scherbatskoy, Jackie Smith, Margaret Stuart, Mariane Tarrant, Lesley Taylor and Rosemary Wilkes. However, the main tribute is to all the makers across Scotland who continue to uphold the traditional craft skills of this fine country.

LIST OF SPONSORS

The support of CALEDONIAN MACBRAYNE LIMITED, P&O SCOTTISH FERRIES LIMITED, PYRAMID, FUJI PHOTO FILM (UK) and KJP has been very much appreciated.